contents

curry basics

Although the word "curry" originally derives from an Indian word, the curries in this book come from a number of different countries, and each region has its own particular basic ingredients that have come to be identified with a particular cuisine. On these pages, we illustrate some of the most commonly used curry ingredients.

coconut

In one of its many forms, coconut appears in many curries, especially those of South-East Asia and in the seafood curries of southern India and Sri Lanka. Coconut can be bought as mature nuts (they should be brown and a bit hairy, not smooth and green), dried, desiccated, shredded or flaked.

Coconut cream is available in cans and tetra packs in supermarkets and Asian stores; coconut milk can be substituted but it is not as thick.

Coconut milk (which should *not* be confused with the liquid inside the mature coconut) can be bought in cans but is also easy to make using desiccated coconut or grated fresh coconut. (Special graters are available from Asian markets and kitchenware shops.) Place 2 cups desiccated or grated fresh coconut in large bowl; cover with 2½ cups hot water. Cover; stand until mixture is just warm. Mix by hand, or process in a blender for about 20 seconds, then strain through a fine sieve or cloth, squeezing out as much liquid as you can. This will give about 1½ cups thick milk; it can be used when canned coconut cream is specified. The same coconut can be used again; simply add another 2½ cups hot water and continue as above; this will give you a watery milk.

It can be combined with the first, thicker milk as a substitute for the canned coconut milk specified in our recipes.

Coconut milk powder is available from supermarkets; follow packet directions to reconstitute. It is a good substitute for coconut milk, but does not deliver the richness of coconut cream.

Light coconut milk Both coconut milk and coconut cream are available in fat-reduced versions, containing up to 50% less fat. Useful for those who need to watch their cholesterol intake, light coconut milk doesn't taste as rich as the full-fat products.

SHREDDED COCONUT

DESICCATED COCONUT

MATURE COCONUT

FLAKED COCONUT

Trident PREMIUM QUALITY Coconut Cream 400ml

asia (at) home™ coconut milk

AYAM BRAND LIGHT Coconut Cream NET 270ml

Trident Lite Coconut Milk 60% LESS FAT

Royal COCONUT MILK UNSWEETENED 400 ml

BLUE DRAGON JUST ADD WARM WATER COCONUT POWDER Coconut powder with added dextrin 160 g

THE AUSTRALIAN Women's Weekly

Not all curries are hot – some are just deliciously spicy, and it's easy to vary the heat to suit individual tastes simply by adjusting the ingredient that makes a curry hot (usually chilli or chilli powder). It's customary to serve rice with curry and to serve all courses together on the table at the same time. Don't forget breads and side dishes – they're what make a curry sing. Some commonly used ingredients are pictured and explained on pages 4-5 and there's a glossary at the back.

Pamela Clark

Food Director

chillies

Like onions and garlic, chillies are an essential ingredient in curry cooking, although not all curries are necessarily mouth-numbingly hot. Chillies are available in many different types and sizes. The tiny ones (birdseye chillies) are the hottest. As fresh chillies can burn your skin, use tight rubber gloves when chopping them. The seeds and membranes are the hottest parts, so remove them if you want to reduce the heat quotient of the finished dish.

If you do not have fresh chillies, you can add heat to a curry by adding a little sambal oelek (a fiery paste made from ground chilli and salt) at the end of cooking. Start with 1/2 teaspoon until you are sure of how hot it is. Fresh chillies can be stored whole in the freezer then chopped when needed, without thawing.

ginger

Ginger is a basic ingredient in both Indian and South-East Asian curries.

Fresh, green or root ginger can be prepared by scraping away the outside skin and grating, chopping or slicing as required. Fresh peeled ginger can be preserved with enough dry sherry to cover; keep in a jar in the refrigerator – it will keep for months. You can also store whole, peeled pieces of ginger in the freezer and grate them while still frozen, as needed. Do not substitute ground dry ginger for fresh in any recipe.

ghee
clarified butter

A pure butter fat that lends a distinctive taste to Indian curries. It can be heated to high temperatures without burning because of the lack of salt and milk solids.

coriander

A strongly flavoured herb also known as cilantro and Chinese parsley, fresh coriander is a popular and distinctive curry ingredient, particularly in the cuisine of South-East Asia. The dried seeds of the coriander plant are also used whole or ground, but are not a substitute for the fresh leaves. Dried coriander is a common ingredient in Indian, Sri Lankan, Malaysian and Indonesian curries.

lemon grass

An important ingredient in Thai and Vietnamese cooking, fresh lemon grass is available from Asian food stores and from most supermarkets. It needs to be bruised or chopped before using to release the flavour. Fresh lemon grass will keep in a jug of water at room temperature for several weeks; the water must be changed daily. Stalks of lemon grass can also be trimmed, ready to use, then simply stored in the freezer until needed. Chopped lemon grass is available in bottles in the spice section of many supermarkets.

FRESH LEMON GRASS

BOTTLED LEMON GRASS

CORIANDER

GINGER

GARLIC

BROWN ONION

PURE GHEE

CORIANDER SEEDS

BIRDSEYE CHILLI

CHILLI

curry blends and pastes

Curry pastes and curry powders are convenient blends of spices in paste and powdered form that are available commercially, although they are seldom used in countries where curries are eaten daily. There, the spices are ground separately and combined according to the curry being prepared.

musaman curry paste

PREPARATION TIME 15 MINUTES

4 small fresh red chillies, seeded, chopped
4 cloves garlic, quartered
3 green onions, chopped
2 teaspoons chopped fresh lemon grass
2 teaspoons peanut oil
2 teaspoons sugar
1/2 teaspoon ground cumin
1/2 teaspoon ground cardamom
1/4 teaspoon ground cinnamon
1/4 teaspoon ground cloves
1/4 teaspoon ground turmeric
2 tablespoons water

Blend or process ingredients until combined. Add a little more water, if necessary, to make a paste.

MAKES ABOUT 1/3 CUP

per tablespoon 2.8g fat; 165kJ

tip Paste can be made a week ahead; store, in airtight container, in refrigerator.

garam masala

PREPARATION TIME 10 MINUTES

2 tablespoons cumin seeds
1 tablespoon black peppercorns
2 teaspoons cloves
2 tablespoons coriander seeds
2 teaspoons caraway seeds
1 1/2 teaspoons cardamom seeds
1 cinnamon stick
1/2 nutmeg, cracked

Combine ingredients in small saucepan; stir over medium heat for about 2 minutes or until fragrant. Blend or process mixture until fine.

MAKES ABOUT 1/2 CUP

per tablespoon 1.7g fat; 152kJ

tip Recipe can be made 2 months ahead; store, in airtight container, in refrigerator.

green masala paste

PREPARATION TIME 15 MINUTES

2 teaspoons fenugreek seeds
2 tablespoons grated fresh ginger
1 teaspoon ground turmeric
3/4 teaspoon ground cloves
3 cloves garlic, quartered
1 1/4 cups firmly packed fresh coriander leaves
1 cup firmly packed fresh mint
1 1/2 teaspoons ground cardamom
1/2 cup brown vinegar (125ml)
1/4 cup vegetable oil (60ml)
1 tablespoon sesame oil

Place seeds in small bowl; cover with boiling water. Stand for 10 minutes; drain. Blend or process seeds, ginger, turmeric, cloves, garlic, coriander, mint, cardamom and vinegar until combined. Heat oils in small saucepan; stir in coriander mixture. Bring to boil; remove from heat, cool.

MAKES ABOUT 1 CUP

per tablespoon 12.3g fat; 475kJ

tip Paste can be made 1 month ahead; store, in airtight container, in refrigerator.

KASHMIRI-STYLE GARAM MASALA

GREEN MASALA PASTE

RED CURRY PASTE

madras-style curry paste

PREPARATION TIME 15 MINUTES

2 teaspoons ground black pepper
3 teaspoons chilli powder
1/2 teaspoon ground cinnamon
2 teaspoons garam masala
2 teaspoons ground turmeric
1/2 cup ground coriander
2 teaspoons black mustard seeds
1/4 cup ground cumin
3 cloves garlic, crushed
2 teaspoons grated fresh ginger
1/2 cup brown vinegar (125ml)
1/3 cup vegetable oil (80ml)

Combine pepper, chilli, cinnamon, garam masala, turmeric, coriander, seeds, cumin, garlic and ginger in medium bowl. Stir in vinegar, mix to a smooth paste. Heat oil in medium saucepan; stir in paste. Stir over low heat until mixture boils and oil begins to separate from spices; remove from heat, cool.

MAKES ABOUT 3/4 CUP

per tablespoon 9.8g fat; 423kJ

tip Paste can be made 1 month ahead; store, in airtight container, in refrigerator.

tandoori mix

PREPARATION TIME 5 MINUTES

1 1/2 tablespoons ground turmeric
3 teaspoons hot paprika
3 teaspoons garam masala
1 1/2 teaspoons ground cardamom
1 teaspoon chilli powder
1/4 teaspoon saffron powder

Combine ingredients in jar; shake until combined.

MAKES ABOUT 1/4 CUP

per tablespoon 1.7g fat; 155kJ

tip Recipe can be made 2 months ahead; store, in airtight container, in refrigerator.

red curry paste

PREPARATION TIME 15 MINUTES

6 dried red chillies, chopped
2 medium brown onions (300g), chopped
3 cloves garlic, crushed
2 tablespoons peanut oil
1 teaspoon grated lemon rind
2 teaspoons shrimp paste
1 tablespoon ground cumin
1 tablespoon hot paprika
2 teaspoons ground turmeric
1 teaspoon ground black pepper

Blend or process ingredients until they form a smooth paste.

MAKES ABOUT 3/4 CUP

per tablespoon 5g fat; 248kJ

tip Recipe can be made 1 week ahead; store, in airtight container, in refrigerator.

kashmiri-style garam masala

PREPARATION TIME 10 MINUTES

2 teaspoons black peppercorns
1 teaspoon cloves
2 teaspoons cumin seeds
3 teaspoons cardamom seeds
1/2 small nutmeg, cracked
2 cinnamon sticks

Place ingredients on oven tray; bake, uncovered, in moderate oven for 5 minutes. Blend or process until finely ground.

MAKES ABOUT 1/4 CUP

per tablespoon 1.5g fat; 134kJ

tip Recipe can be made 1 month ahead; store, in airtight container, in refrigerator.

TANDOORI MIX

MUSAMAN CURRY PASTE

MADRAS-STYLE CURRY PASTE

GARAM MASALA

appetisers

Many different types of morsels from Asia and India can be eaten with the fingers. They are ideal to serve at any type of party and before dinner. Several can be served as a mini meal when you don't want to go to the trouble of providing a full-spread buffet.

crisp corn fritters

PREPARATION TIME 15 MINUTES • COOKING TIME 30 MINUTES

4 green onions, chopped
1 trimmed stick celery (75g), chopped finely
1 clove garlic, crushed
130g can corn kernels, drained
1 medium green capsicum (200g), chopped finely
2 eggs
$^1/_2$ teaspoon garam masala
100g king prawns, shelled
2 small fresh red chillies, chopped
2 tablespoons plain flour
2 teaspoons baking powder
oil for shallow-frying

SAUCE
1 tablespoon plain flour
3 teaspoons brown sugar
$^1/_2$ cup water (125ml)
1$^1/_2$ tablespoons dark soy sauce

Adding chilli to food processor

Combining all ingredients

1 Combine onion, celery, garlic, corn and capsicum in large bowl. Blend or process eggs, garam masala, prawns and chilli until smooth.

2 Stir egg mixture, sifted flour and baking powder into vegetable mixture. Spoon rounded tablespoons of mixture into oil; spread into flat rounds. Shallow-fry until golden brown. Remove fritters from oil; drain on absorbent paper. Serve with sauce.

sauce Stir flour in small saucepan over low heat until lightly browned. Stir in sugar; cook over low heat until sugar begins to melt. Gradually stir in the water; stir over high heat until mixture boils and thickens, stir in sauce.

MAKES ABOUT 10

per fritter 6.1g fat; 402kJ

tip Fritters are best made close to serving time.

mini pork kebabs with satay sauce

PREPARATION TIME 20 MINUTES (plus refrigeration time) • COOKING TIME 20 MINUTES

2 medium pork fillets (480g)
1 medium brown
    onion (150g), grated
2 teaspoons grated fresh ginger
2 teaspoons brown sugar
1/2 teaspoon sambal djeroek
1 teaspoon ground coriander
1 tablespoon light soy sauce
1/2 teaspoon ground cumin
2 tablespoons coconut cream

SATAY SAUCE
3/4 cup roasted unsalted
    peanuts (110g)
1 tablespoon sambal oelek
1 tablespoon brown sugar
1 tablespoon light soy sauce
1/4 cup water (60ml)
1/2 cup coconut cream (125ml)
1 teaspoon chopped fresh
    lemon grass

Spreading marinade over kebabs

1 Slice pork into long thin
   strips; thread two strips onto
   each skewer.

2 Combine onion, ginger, sugar,
   sambal, coriander, sauce, cumin
   and coconut cream in small
   bowl; mix well.

3 Place kebabs onto tray, spread
   with marinade; cover, refrigerate
   overnight. Grill or barbecue kebabs
   until golden brown and tender.

4 Serve with hot satay sauce.

   satay sauce Blend or process
   peanuts until finely chopped.
   Combine peanuts with remaining
   ingredients in small saucepan;
   stir over medium heat, without
   boiling, until heated through.

SERVES 6

per serve 16.6g fat; 1185kJ

tip Recipe can be prepared
a day ahead; keep, covered,
in refrigerator. Cook just
before serving.

Kneading dough

Cutting pastry into strips

fried pastry morsels

PREPARATION TIME 15 MINUTES (plus refrigeration time) • COOKING TIME 10 MINUTES

2 cups plain flour (300g)
1/2 teaspoon chilli powder
1/2 teaspoon ground cumin
1 teaspoon cumin seeds
1/2 teaspoon dried thyme
1/4 teaspoon ground ginger
1 teaspoon grated lime rind
1 teaspoon garam masala
60g ghee, melted
1/2 cup water (125ml),
 approximately
oil for deep-frying
1 teaspoon garam masala, extra

1 Combine sifted flour, chilli, ground cumin, cumin seeds, thyme, ginger, rind and garam masala in medium bowl; mix well. Make well in centre; stir in ghee and enough water to mix to a firm dough (or process ingredients until mixture clings together). Turn dough onto floured surface; knead lightly until smooth. Cover; refrigerate dough for 30 minutes.

2 Divide dough into four portions; roll out each portion on floured surface to form a 20cm x 25cm rectangle. Cut pastry into 1cm x 10cm strips. Twist strips into novelty shapes, if desired. Deep-fry strips in hot oil until golden brown and crisp. Toss in extra garam masala before serving.

SERVES 6

per serve 15.3g fat; 1293kJ

tip Recipe can be made several hours ahead; keep in airtight container. Uncooked pastry can be frozen for up to two months.

fish patties with sweet chilli sauce

PREPARATION TIME 20 MINUTES (plus refrigeration time) • COOKING TIME 25 MINUTES

1 small carrot (70g), grated
1 small zucchini (90g), grated
3 green onions, chopped
2 cloves garlic, chopped
1 small fresh red chilli, chopped
2 teaspoons grated fresh ginger
1 tablespoon chopped
   fresh coriander
1 teaspoon grated lime rind
375g boneless white
   fish fillets, chopped
1 tablespoon fish sauce
2/3 cup plain flour (100g)
1 teaspoon ground turmeric
1/4 cup peanut oil (60ml)

SWEET CHILLI SAUCE
1/2 cup white vinegar (125ml)
1 1/2 tablespoons brown sugar
2 small fresh red chillies,
   chopped finely
1 teaspoon cornflour
1/4 cup water (60ml)
1 tablespoon chopped fresh basil
2 teaspoons chopped
   fresh coriander

1 Blend or process carrot, zucchini, onion, garlic, chilli, ginger, coriander and rind until finely chopped. Add fish and sauce; blend or process until well combined.

2 Toss level tablespoons of fish mixture in combined sifted flour and turmeric; shape into patties. Place patties onto plate; refrigerate for 15 minutes. Heat oil in large frying pan; cook patties over medium heat for about 2 minutes on each side or until lightly browned. Remove from pan; drain on absorbent paper. Serve with sauce.

sweet chilli sauce Combine vinegar, sugar and chilli in small saucepan; stir over medium heat until sugar is dissolved. Blend cornflour with the water; stir into vinegar mixture over medium heat, until sauce boils and thickens. Remove from heat; stir in basil and coriander.

MAKES ABOUT 20

per patty 3.6g fat; 311kJ

tip Patties and sauce can be made a day ahead; keep, covered, in refrigerator or freeze for up to a month. We used ling fillets in this recipe.

Adding fish to other chopped ingredients

Shaping fish mixture into patties

Adding coconut milk to mixture

Piping dough into hot oil

rice flour crisps

PREPARATION TIME 10 MINUTES • COOKING TIME 15 MINUTES

1¹/₂ cups rice flour (225g)
¹/₃ cup besan flour (50g)
1 tablespoon cumin seeds
2 teaspoons chilli powder
30g ghee
1 cup coconut milk
    (250ml), approximately
oil for deep-frying

1 Combine sifted flours, seeds and chilli in medium bowl; rub in ghee. Make well in centre; stir in enough coconut milk to form a soft dough.

2 Spoon dough into piping bag fitted with small star tube. Pipe 5cm lengths of dough directly into hot oil; deep-fry until golden brown and crisp. Remove crisps with slotted spoon; drain on absorbent paper. Sprinkle with salt, if desired.

SERVES 6

per serve 19.5g fat; 1449kJ

tip Crisps can be prepared a week ahead; keep in airtight container.

vegetable fritters with yogurt dip

PREPARATION TIME 20 MINUTES • COOKING TIME 20 MINUTES

3/4 cup besan flour (110g)
3/4 cup self-raising flour (110g)
2 cloves garlic, crushed
1 1/2 teaspoons garam masala
1 teaspoon chilli powder
1 teaspoon cumin seeds
1 tablespoon chopped
   fresh coriander
1 cup water (250ml)
1 medium potato (200g),
   chopped finely
1 small eggplant (230g),
   chopped finely
1 medium zucchini (120g),
   chopped finely
250g cauliflower, chopped finely
oil for deep-frying

YOGURT DIP
1 teaspoon cumin seeds
1 cup plain yogurt (250ml)
1 small fresh red chilli, chopped
1/2 teaspoon paprika
2 tablespoons chopped fresh mint
1 tablespoon chopped
   fresh coriander

1 Sift flours into large bowl. Stir in garlic, garam masala, chilli powder, seeds and coriander. Make well in centre, gradually stir in water, mix to a batter; stir in vegetables.

2 Deep-fry heaped tablespoons of vegetable mixture, in batches, in hot oil until golden brown; drain on absorbent paper. Serve hot with dip.

yogurt dip Place seeds in small frying pan, stir over medium heat for about 2 minutes or until fragrant; remove from heat, cool. Combine seeds with remaining ingredients in small bowl; mix well.

MAKES ABOUT 45

per fritter 1.9g fat; 173kJ

tip Fritters are best cooked just before serving. Batter can be made several hours ahead; keep, covered, in refrigerator.

Stirring vegetables into batter

Deep frying vegetable mixture

potato pea pastries

PREPARATION TIME 35 MINUTES (plus cooling time) • COOKING TIME 15 MINUTES

1¹/2 cups plain flour (225g)
1 tablespoon peanut oil
¹/4 cup water (60ml)
2 large potatoes (300g),
    chopped finely
³/4 cup frozen peas (90g), thawed
1 teaspoon ground cumin
¹/2 teaspoon chilli powder
¹/2 teaspoon ground cinnamon
2 tablespoons currants
1 tablespoon chopped
    fresh coriander
2 tablespoons lemon juice
1 tablespoon light soy sauce
oil for deep-frying

1 Sift flour into medium bowl, stir in oil and the water; mix to a soft dough, knead on floured surface until smooth. Cover pastry; refrigerate for 1 hour. Boil, steam or microwave potatoes until tender; drain, cool. Combine potatoes, peas, cumin, chilli and cinnamon in large bowl. Stir in currants, coriander, juice and sauce.

2 Roll out half the pastry, on floured surface, to form a 30cm x 40cm rectangle. Cut pastry into rounds using 10cm cutter. Place a heaped tablespoon of potato mixture on half of each round. Fold rounds in half, pressing edges together with a fork. Repeat with remaining pastry and potato mixture. Deep-fry batches of pastries in hot oil until golden brown. Remove from oil; drain on absorbent paper. Serve hot.

MAKES ABOUT 24

per pastry 2.8g fat; 293kJ

tip Pastries can be prepared a day ahead; keep, covered, in refrigerator or freeze for up to a month. Deep-fry pastries just before serving.

Stirring oil and the water into flour

Placing potato mixture on pastry rounds

savoury nibbles

PREPARATION TIME 10 MINUTES • COOKING TIME 10 MINUTES

2 teaspoons peanut oil
2 cloves garlic, crushed
1 teaspoon coriander seeds
1 teaspoon black mustard seeds
2 teaspoons sambal oelek
1/2 teaspoon ground cinnamon
1/4 teaspoon ground cloves
1/4 teaspoon ground nutmeg
3/4 teaspoon chilli powder
1 cup besan flour (150g)
1 cup self-raising flour (150g)
1 cup warm water (250ml)
1/2 cup buttermilk (125ml)
oil for deep-frying

Stirring buttermilk and water into flour

Dripping batter into oil

1 Heat oil in small saucepan; cook garlic, seeds, sambal, cinnamon, cloves, nutmeg and chilli. Stir over medium heat for about 2 minutes or until fragrant. Remove mixture from heat; crush with mortar and pestle or blend until finely ground. Sift flours into medium bowl, make well in centre; gradually stir in combined water and buttermilk, then spice mixture. Mix to a smooth batter.

2 Heat oil in medium saucepan. Place large spoonfuls of batter onto large perforated spoon. Holding perforated spoon over oil, tap edge so batter drips through holes and into hot oil. Cook batter drops until golden brown, remove from oil using slotted spoon; drain on absorbent paper. Sprinkle with salt, if desired.

SERVES 4

per serve 14.3g fat; 1675kJ

tip Nibbles can be made 2 hours ahead; keep in an airtight container.

sesame fish balls

PREPARATION TIME 30 MINUTES (plus refrigeration and cooling time) • COOKING TIME 20 MINUTES

**500g boneless white
fish fillets, chopped**
**1¹/₂ cups stale
breadcrumbs (150g)**
¹/₄ cup plain yogurt (60ml)
2 eggs, separated
**1 small brown onion (80g),
chopped finely**
1 clove garlic, crushed
1 teaspoon grated fresh ginger
¹/₂ teaspoon ground cumin
¹/₄ teaspoon chilli powder
**2 tablespoons chopped
fresh coriander**
**1 cup packaged
breadcrumbs (100g)**
¹/₄ cup sesame seeds (35g)
oil for deep-frying

1 Steam, poach or microwave fish until tender; cool to room temperature. Process fish until smooth. Transfer fish to large bowl; stir in combined stale breadcrumbs, yogurt, egg yolks, onion, garlic, ginger, cumin, chilli and coriander; mix well.

2 Shape mixture into 24 balls, dip into lightly beaten egg whites; coat balls firmly with combined packaged breadcrumbs and seed, refrigerate on tray for 30 minutes. Deep-fry balls in hot oil until golden brown; drain on absorbent paper.

MAKES 24

per fish ball 4.6g fat; 366kJ
tip Recipe can be prepared a day ahead; keep, covered, in refrigerator or freeze for up to a month. Cook close to serving time.

Stirring breadcrumb mixture into fish

Deep-frying balls in oil

chicken picks

PREPARATION TIME 1 HOUR 10 MINUTES (plus refrigeration time)
COOKING TIME 15 MINUTES

3kg chicken wings
3 cloves garlic, crushed
1 teaspoon chopped fresh ginger
2 tablespoons light soy sauce
1/4 cup lime juice (60ml)
2 tablespoons sugar
2 tablespoons peanut oil
1/2 teaspoon chilli powder
1 teaspoon ground coriander
1 tablespoon chopped fresh coriander
1/2 cup coconut cream (125ml)
1 teaspoon cornflour
1 tablespoon water

Scraping meat to end of bones

Adding coconut cream to chicken mixture

1 Cut first and second joints from wings. Holding small end of third joint, trim around bone with sharp knife. Cut, scrape and push meat down to large end. Using fingers, pull skin and meat over end of bone; they will resemble baby drumsticks.

2 Blend or process garlic, ginger, sauce, juice, sugar, oil, chilli and ground coriander until mixture is smooth. Pour mixture over chicken pieces in large bowl. Stir in fresh coriander and coconut cream, cover; refrigerate for several hours or overnight.

3 Grill or barbecue chicken until well browned and tender; brush with marinade occasionally during cooking. Place remaining marinade into small saucepan. Blend cornflour with the water, stir into marinade; stir over high heat until mixture boils and thickens. Serve as a dipping sauce with chicken.

MAKES ABOUT 30

per chicken pick 8.1g fat; 485kJ

tip Leftover chicken can be used for stock. Recipe is best prepared a day ahead; keep, covered, in refrigerator or freeze for up to a month. Cook chicken just before serving.

pork bundles with coriander sauce

PREPARATION TIME 1 HOUR 15 MINUTES (plus standing time) • COOKING TIME 1 HOUR

1¹/₄ cups plain flour (185g)
2 teaspoons cornflour
¹/₂ cup boiling water (125ml)
2 teaspoons vegetable oil

FILLING

8 dried shiitake mushrooms
400g pork fillets, minced
2 tablespoons dry sherry
1 tablespoon water
1 clove garlic, crushed
2 teaspoons grated fresh ginger
2 teaspoons cornflour
1 medium carrot (120g), grated
2 tablespoons oyster sauce
2 teaspoons light soy sauce

CORIANDER SAUCE

1 tablespoon cornflour
1¹/₄ cups water (310ml)
1 teaspoon grated fresh ginger
2 teaspoons chopped
   fresh coriander
1 small fresh red chilli,
   chopped finely
1 clove garlic, crushed
1¹/₂ teaspoons sugar
1 chicken stock cube, crumbled
1 teaspoon lime juice
1 teaspoon light soy sauce

1 Sift flours into medium bowl, make well in centre; gradually add combined boiling water and oil, mix to a pliable dough. Cover dough, stand 10 minutes; turn onto floured surface, knead until smooth, cover dough.

2 Divide dough into 48 portions. Roll one portion of dough out thinly, on floured surface, to form a 6cm circle. Place a heaped teaspoon of filling in centre of circle. Shape pastry around mixture as shown below. Repeat with remaining dough and filling.

3 Place bundles, about 1cm apart, in lightly greased bamboo steamer. Cover, steam over simmering water for about 5 minutes or until filling is cooked through. Serve with sauce.

filling Place mushrooms in medium bowl, cover with boiling water; stand for 20 minutes, drain. Discard stems; chop mushrooms finely. Combine mince, sherry, the water, garlic, ginger, cornflour, carrot, mushrooms and sauces in medium bowl; mix well.

coriander sauce Blend cornflour with the water in small saucepan; stir in ginger, coriander, chilli, garlic, sugar, stock cube, juice and sauce. Stir over medium heat until mixture boils and thickens. Use while hot.

MAKES 48

per bundle 0.4g fat; 121kJ

tip Bundles can be made several hours ahead; keep, covered, in refrigerator. Filling can be frozen for up to two months. Sauce and pastry unsuitable to freeze.

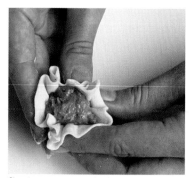

Shaping pastry around mixture

mini spring rolls

PREPARATION TIME 50 MINUTES (plus cooling time) • COOKING TIME 25 MINUTES

200g can bamboo shoots, drained
2 trimmed sticks celery (150g)
2 medium carrots (240g)
1 tablespoon peanut oil
1 clove garlic, crushed
1 small fresh red chilli,
  chopped finely
1/2 teaspoon sambal oelek
50 small spring roll wrappers
1 egg white, beaten lightly
oil for deep-frying

DIPPING SAUCE

1 teaspoon sambal oelek
1 teaspoon grated fresh ginger
1 clove garlic, crushed
1 tablespoon chopped fresh basil
2 teaspoons chopped
  fresh coriander
2 tablespoons cider vinegar
1 tablespoon brown sugar

1 Cut bamboo shoots, celery and carrots into thin strips about 5cm long. Heat oil in medium frying pan; cook garlic, chilli and vegetables, stirring, over medium heat for about 3 minutes or until vegetables are soft. Stir in sambal; cool to room temperature.

2 Place a heaped tablespoon of vegetable mixture on one side of a spring roll wrapper; brush edges with egg white, fold sides in, brush ends lightly with egg white, roll up firmly. Repeat with remaining mixture, wrappers and egg white. Deep-fry rolls in hot oil until golden brown; drain on absorbent paper. Serve with dipping sauce.

dipping sauce Combine ingredients in small bowl; mix well.

MAKES 50

per roll 1.4g fat; 87kJ

tip Spring rolls can be prepared several hours ahead; keep, covered with a damp cloth, in refrigerator. Deep-fry rolls just before serving. Uncooked rolls can be frozen for a month.

Adding chopped vegetables to pan

Brushing wrapper edges with egg white

spicy mince bites with mint chutney

PREPARATION TIME 40 MINUTES (plus refrigeration and cooling time) • COOKING TIME 20 MINUTES

30g ghee
1 medium brown onion (150g),
chopped finely
2 cloves garlic, crushed
1 small red capsicum (150g),
chopped finely
2 tablespoons chopped
fresh coriander
2 teaspoons ground ginger
1/2 teaspoon chilli powder
1/4 teaspoon ground turmeric
500g minced beef
1 medium tomato (190g),
peeled, chopped
2 tablespoons yellow split peas
1 cup water (250ml)
2 tablespoons plain flour
2 teaspoons ground allspice
2 tablespoons lemon juice
oil for deep-frying

BATTER
1/3 cup besan flour (50g)
1/2 cup milk (125ml)

MINT CHUTNEY
1/4 cup chutney (85g)
1 tablespoon lemon juice
1 tablespoon brown sugar
1 tablespoon chopped fresh mint

1 Melt ghee in large frying pan; cook onion, garlic, capsicum, coriander, ginger, chilli and turmeric, stirring, over high heat for about 2 minutes or until onion is soft. Add mince; stir over high heat for about 2 minutes or until mince is browned all over. Stir in tomato, peas and the water, bring to a boil; reduce heat, cover, simmer for about 45 minutes or until all liquid has evaporated, stirring occasionally.

2 Remove mixture from heat; stir in flour, allspice and juice, cool slightly. Process mixture until smooth, transfer to large bowl; refrigerate 30 minutes. Mould mixture into 24 ovals, dip into batter; carefully lower into hot oil. Deep-fry, in batches, until golden brown; drain on absorbent paper. Serve with chutney.

batter Sift flour into medium bowl; make well in centre. Gradually whisk in milk; whisk until smooth.

mint chutney Blend or process ingredients until smooth.

MAKES 24

per bite 6.4g fat; 446kJ

tip Bites can be prepared a day ahead; keep, covered, in refrigerator. Coat bites in batter and deep-fry just before serving.

Stirring the water into mixture

Lowering ovals into hot oil

pork and veal parcels with tamarind sauce

PREPARATION TIME 35 MINUTES (plus standing and cooling time) • COOKING TIME 25 MINUTES

2 trimmed sticks celery (150g)
2 teaspoons peanut oil
500g pork and veal mince
1 medium brown onion (150g),
    chopped finely
2 cloves garlic, crushed
2 medium fresh red
    chillies, chopped
1 teaspoon cracked
    black peppercorns
1 tablespoon plain flour
1 cup chopped fresh coriander
20 small spring roll wrappers
oil for deep-frying

TAMARIND SAUCE

1 tablespoon tamarind concentrate
2/3 cup water (160ml)
2 teaspoons ground coriander
1 tablespoon sugar
2 teaspoons chopped
    fresh coriander

1 Use vegetable peeler to cut ribbons from celery. Cut ribbons into thin strips; place in small bowl of hot water for about 15 minutes or until soft.

2 Heat oil in medium saucepan; cook mince, onion, garlic, chilli and peppercorns, stirring, over medium heat for about 10 minutes or until mince is browned. Stir in flour and coriander; cool to room temperature. Place a level tablespoon of mince mixture onto the centre of each wrapper. Pull up edges into a parcel, as shown below; secure with celery string. Deep-fry parcels, in batches, in hot oil until lightly browned; drain on absorbent paper. Serve parcels with sauce.

tamarind sauce Combine ingredients in medium bowl; mix well.

MAKES 20

per parcel 6.9g fat; 441kJ
tip Parcels are best cooked close to serving time.

Cutting celery ribbons into thin strips

Pulling up edges into a parcel

tamarind lamb balls

PREPARATION TIME 40 MINUTES (plus standing time) • COOKING TIME 30 MINUTES

4 dried shiitake mushrooms
500g minced lamb
1 medium brown onion
(150g), chopped
1 medium carrot (120g), grated
2 green onions, chopped
1 tablespoon chopped fresh
lemon grass
1 clove garlic, crushed
1 tablespoon light soy sauce
3/4 cup sesame seeds (110g)
oil for deep-frying

TAMARIND SAUCE
1 tablespoon tomato sauce
2 tablespoons light soy sauce
1 tablespoon tamarind sauce
2 tablespoons dry sherry
2 teaspoons honey
1/4 cup water (60ml)
2 teaspoons cornflour
1 tablespoon water, extra

1 Place mushrooms in small bowl, cover with boiling water, stand for 20 minutes; drain, discard stems, chop mushrooms finely. Combine mince, brown onion, carrot, green onion, lemon grass, garlic, mushrooms and sauce in large bowl; mix well. Shape mixture into 2cm balls. Toss balls in sesame seeds.

2 Deep-fry balls in hot oil until golden brown; drain on absorbent paper. Serve hot with sauce.

tamarind sauce Combine sauces, sherry, honey and the water in small saucepan. Blend cornflour with the extra water; stir into sauce mixture. Stir over high heat until sauce boils and thickens. Serve hot.

MAKES ABOUT 40

per ball 4.8g fat; 256kJ

tip Recipe can be made a day ahead; keep, covered, in refrigerator or freeze for up to two months. Minced lamb can be ordered ahead from your butcher.

Combining ingredients in bowl

meat

There is quite a lot of difference between the curries of India and South-East Asia. While the Asians use coconut milk as a thickener and many citrus ingredients, the Indians tend to use yogurt and crushed nuts as thickeners. You will find a wide variety of recipes in this section and, in most cases, one meat can be substituted for another.

fried pork curry

PREPARATION TIME 20 MINUTES (plus standing time) • COOKING TIME 1 HOUR 10 MINUTES

40g tamarind pulp
2¹/₂ cups boiling water (625ml)
750g pork fillets
¹/₄ cup peanut oil (60ml)
2 medium brown onions
   (300g), chopped
2 cloves garlic, crushed
10 dried curry leaves
¹/₂ teaspoon fenugreek seeds
2 teaspoons grated fresh ginger
1¹/₂ teaspoons curry powder
¹/₂ teaspoon chilli powder
1 tablespoon white vinegar
2 tablespoons chutney
1 cinnamon stick
4 cardamom pods
1 cup coconut milk (250ml)

1 Combine tamarind pulp and the water in small bowl; stand for 1 hour. Squeeze liquid from pulp, strain mixture; reserve liquid, discard pulp.

2 Cut pork into 2cm slices.

3 Heat oil in large saucepan; cook onion, garlic, leaves, seeds and ginger, stirring, over medium heat for about 3 minutes or until onions are soft. Stir in curry powder and chilli powder.

4 Add pork gradually to pan in single layer; stir constantly over medium heat for about 5 minutes, or until pork is lightly browned all over.

5 Stir in vinegar, chutney, cinnamon stick, cardamom pods and reserved tamarind liquid; bring to a boil. Reduce heat; simmer, covered, for about 45 minutes or until pork is tender.

6 Stir in coconut milk; cook over medium heat, uncovered, for about 10 minutes or until mixture thickens.

SERVES 4

per serve 32.2g fat; 2212kJ

tip Recipe can be made a day ahead; keep, covered, in refrigerator or freeze for up to 2 months.

Combining tamarind pulp and the water

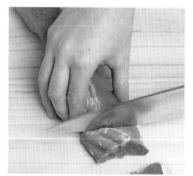
Cutting pork into 2cm slices

Adding curry powder to saucepan

lamb curry with coconut cream

PREPARATION TIME 20 MINUTES (plus refrigeration time) • COOKING TIME 1 HOUR 25 MINUTES

Ask your butcher to bone the leg of lamb for you.

**1 medium brown onion
   (150g), chopped**
2 cloves garlic, crushed
**1/4 cup shelled pistachio
   nuts (35g)**
1/4 cup coconut cream (60ml)
2.5kg leg of lamb, boned, cubed
2 tablespoons peanut oil
**1 medium brown onion (150g),
   chopped, extra**
**1 tablespoon chopped
   fresh lemon grass**
2 teaspoons ground coriander
1 teaspoon ground cumin
1 teaspoon ground ginger
3 cardamom pods
2 tablespoons tamarind sauce
**1 1/4 cups coconut cream
   (310ml), extra**
1 teaspoon plain flour
1 tablespoon water
**2 tablespoons chopped
   fresh coriander**

1 Blend or process onion, garlic, nuts and coconut cream until smooth. Combine onion mixture and lamb in large bowl, stir until lamb is well coated, cover; refrigerate for several hours or overnight.

2 Heat oil in large saucepan; cook extra onion, stir over heat for about 2 minutes or until onion is soft. Add lemon grass, ground coriander, cumin, ginger and cardamom pods; stir over heat for 2 minutes.

3 Stir in lamb mixture; cook over high heat for about 5 minutes or until lamb is browned all over. Stir in sauce and extra coconut cream. Bring to boil, reduce heat; simmer, covered, for 30 minutes. Remove cover; simmer further 30 minutes or until lamb is tender, stirring occasionally.

4 Blend flour with the water; stir into lamb mixture over high heat until mixture boils and thickens. Stir in fresh coriander just before serving.

SERVES 6

per serve 29g fat; 2486kJ

tip Curry can be made 2 days ahead; keep, covered, in refrigerator or freeze for up to 2 months.

Pouring coconut cream into blender

Adding lemon grass to saucepan

very dry beef curry

PREPARATION TIME 15 MINUTES • COOKING TIME 1 HOUR 50 MINUTES

2 tablespoons peanut oil
2 large brown onions
   (400g), chopped
3 cloves garlic, crushed
1 tablespoon grated fresh ginger
1 teaspoon ground turmeric
1/2 teaspoon chilli powder
2 tablespoons chopped
   fresh lemon grass
1.5kg chuck steak, cubed
1 1/4 cups water (310ml)

1 Heat oil in large frying pan; cook onion, garlic, ginger, turmeric, chilli and lemon grass, stirring over heat for 3 minutes or until onions are soft.

2 Stir in steak; cook over high heat for about 5 minutes or until steak is browned all over.

3 Stir in the water, bring to a boil; reduce heat, simmer, covered, for about 1 1/2 hours or until steak is tender.

4 Remove lid, stir over high heat until liquid has evaporated.

SERVES 4

per serve 20.7g fat; 2189kJ
tip Curry is best made just before serving.

Adding garlic and ginger to frying pan

Stirring in steak

Pouring water into pan

Tossing lamb kofta in flour

Deep-frying kofta in batches

lamb kofta in yogurt sauce

PREPARATION TIME 30 MINUTES • COOKING TIME 25 MINUTES

1kg lean boneless lamb
1 teaspoon garam masala
1 egg
2 tablespoons cornflour
2 tablespoons plain flour
oil for deep-frying
60g ghee
2 medium brown onions
   (300g), sliced
2 teaspoons finely chopped
   fresh ginger
1 teaspoon ground cumin
1/4 teaspoon ground cinnamon
1/4 teaspoon ground cloves
1 teaspoon cardamom seeds
1/3 cup besan flour (50g)
11/2 cups water (375ml)
2 cups plain yogurt (500ml)
2 tablespoons desiccated coconut
2 tablespoons chopped fresh
   flat-leaf parsley
2 teaspoons chopped fresh mint

1 Trim excess fat from lamb. Process lamb, garam masala, egg and cornflour until smooth. Roll heaped tablespoons of mixture into ovals; toss in plain flour.

2 Deep-fry kofta, in batches, in hot oil for about 2 minutes or until kofta are just beginning to brown; drain on absorbent paper.

3 Melt ghee in medium saucepan. Cook onion, ginger, cumin, cinnamon, cloves and seeds, stirring, over medium heat for about 3 minutes (or microwave on HIGH for about 4 minutes) or until onions are soft. Add flour; stir over medium heat for 2 minutes (or microwave on HIGH for 2 minutes). Remove from heat; gradually stir in combined water and yogurt. Stir over high heat (or microwave on HIGH for about 3 minutes) until mixture boils and thickens.

4 Add kofta to saucepan; stir in coconut. Simmer, partly covered, for about 5 minutes or until kofta are cooked through. Stir in parsley and mint just before serving.

SERVES 4

per serve 47.8g fat; 3426kJ

tip Lamb mixture can be prepared 2 days ahead; keep, covered, in refrigerator. Recipe can be cooked a day ahead; keep, covered, in refrigerator.

braised lamb and yogurt

PREPARATION TIME 20 MINUTES (plus refrigeration time) • COOKING TIME 1 HOUR 15 MINUTES

Ask your butcher to bone the leg of lamb for you.

1 medium brown onion
   (150g), chopped
1 tablespoon grated fresh ginger
2 cloves garlic, crushed
1 teaspoon coriander seeds
1 teaspoon cumin seeds
1/2 teaspoon cardamom seeds
2 tablespoons lime juice
2.5kg leg of lamb, boned, chopped
30g ghee
1/4 teaspoon cayenne pepper
2 teaspoons ground turmeric
1 teaspoon garam masala
2/3 cup plain yogurt (160ml)
2/3 cup cream (160ml)
1 cup water (250ml)
1 tablespoon plain flour
2 tablespoons water, extra
400g can chickpeas,
   rinsed, drained
2 medium tomatoes
   (380g), chopped
1 tablespoon chopped
   fresh parsley

1 Blend or process onion, ginger, garlic, seeds and juice until well combined. Place blended mixture and lamb in medium bowl, stir until lamb is well coated, cover; refrigerate for several hours or overnight.

2 Heat ghee in large saucepan, add cayenne pepper, turmeric and garam masala; stir over medium heat for 1 minute.

3 Stir in yogurt, then lamb; stir over high heat until lamb is well browned. Stir in combined cream and water, bring to a boil, reduce heat; simmer, uncovered, for about 1 hour or until lamb is tender. Stir in chickpeas and tomato.

4 Stir in blended flour and the extra water; stir over high heat until sauce boils and thickens. Serve sprinkled with parsley.

SERVES 6

per serve 22.9g fat; 2223kJ

tip Recipe can be made a day ahead; keep, covered, in refrigerator.

Adding ginger and garlic to blender

Heating ghee in pan

Pouring yogurt into ghee mixture

musaman beef curry

PREPARATION TIME 25 MINUTES (plus cooling time) • COOKING TIME 1 HOUR 10 MINUTES

1kg topside steak
1/4 cup peanut oil (60ml)
500g small potatoes, halved
250g small brown onions, halved
2 x 400ml cans coconut cream
1 teaspoon tamarind concentrate
2/3 cup hot water (160ml)
1/4 cup brown sugar (50g)

MUSAMAN CURRY PASTE
3 green onions, chopped
2 cloves garlic, crushed
2 tablespoons chopped
  fresh lemon grass
2 red Thai chillies, chopped
1 tablespoon coriander seeds
1 tablespoon cumin seeds
3 cardamom pods
1/2 teaspoon ground nutmeg
1/4 teaspoon ground cloves
1/4 teaspoon black peppercorns
2 teaspoons shrimp paste
2 tablespoons warm water

1 Cut steak into 3cm cubes. Heat oil in large saucepan; cook steak, stirring, over high heat until steak is browned all over. Remove steak from pan; drain on absorbent paper.

2 Add potato and onion to same pan; stir over high heat until lightly browned. Stir in musaman curry paste; stir over heat 1 minute.

3 Stir in coconut cream, then stir in steak, combined tamarind concentrate, the water and sugar, bring to a boil; reduce heat, simmer, uncovered, for about 45 minutes or until meat is tender and mixture has thickened.

musaman curry paste Combine onion, garlic, lemon grass, chilli, seeds, cardamom pods, nutmeg, cloves and peppercorns in small bowl, sprinkle onto oven tray; bake in moderate oven for 10 minutes, cool. Blend or process shrimp paste and the water until combined. Add spice mixture a few spoonfuls at a time; blend or process until finely chopped.

SERVES 6

per serve 42.6g fat; 2743kJ

tip Curry can be made 2 days ahead; keep, covered, in refrigerator or freeze for up to 2 months. Curry paste will keep, covered, in refrigerator for 2 weeks.

Browning steak in saucepan

Adding paste to onion and potato

Combining steak with other ingredients

Stirring water into mixture

beef and yogurt with tomatoes

PREPARATION TIME 20 MINUTES (plus refrigeration time) • COOKING TIME 2 HOURS 10 MINUTES

1kg chuck steak, cubed
1 teaspoon finely chopped
   fresh ginger
2 cloves garlic, crushed
2 cinnamon sticks
2 cardamom pods, bruised
1 teaspoon chilli powder
1 teaspoon cumin seeds
1 teaspoon garam masala
200g carton plain yogurt
1/2 cup peanut oil (125ml)
3 medium brown onions
   (450g), sliced
2 cups water (500ml)
2 medium tomatoes
   (380g), chopped
2 tablespoons lemon juice
1/2 cup chopped fresh coriander

1 Combine steak, ginger, garlic, cinnamon sticks, cardamom pods, chilli, seeds and garam masala in large bowl; mix well.

2 Stir in yogurt; cover, refrigerate for several hours or overnight.

3 Heat oil in large saucepan; cook onions, stirring, over medium heat for about 4 minutes or until onions are soft. Stir in steak mixture, over high heat, until steak is well browned.

4 Stir in the water, bring to a boil, reduce heat; simmer, uncovered, for about 2 hours or until steak is tender. Stir tomato, juice and coriander into pan over medium heat for 2 minutes.

SERVES 4

per serve 39.2g fat, 2601kJ

tip Recipe is best made close to serving time.

devil's pork curry

PREPARATION TIME 15 MINUTES (plus standing time) • COOKING TIME 1 HOUR

750g diced pork
1 tablespoon white vinegar
2 tablespoons light soy sauce
2 tablespoons peanut oil
2 medium red onions
  (340g), sliced
1 tablespoon chopped fresh ginger
2 cloves garlic, crushed
12 dried curry leaves
1 teaspoon brown sugar
1 cinnamon stick
1 teaspoon fenugreek seeds
4 small fresh red chillies,
  chopped finely
1/2 teaspoon ground turmeric
1 tablespoon chopped fresh
  lemon grass
1 teaspoon tamarind concentrate
2 teaspoons fish sauce
1 cup beef stock (250ml)
1/3 cup macadamia nuts (50g),
  chopped finely

1 Combine pork, vinegar and sauce in medium bowl, mix well; stand for 20 minutes. Drain pork; reserve liquid.

2 Heat oil in large frying pan; stir in onion, ginger, garlic, curry leaves, sugar, cinnamon stick, seeds, chilli, turmeric and lemon grass. Stir over medium heat for about 5 minutes or until onions are soft.

3 Add pork to onion mixture; stir over high heat until pork is browned.

4 Transfer mixture to medium saucepan; stir in combined tamarind concentrate, fish sauce, stock, nuts and reserved liquid. Stir over high heat until mixture boils, reduce heat; simmer, covered, for 15 minutes. Remove lid, simmer for about 30 minutes or until most of the liquid has evaporated; remove cinnamon stick before serving.

SERVES 4

per serve 22.4g fat; 1757kJ

tip Curry can be made 3 days ahead; keep, covered, in refrigerator or freeze for up to 2 months.

Adding soy sauce to pork

Stirring onion mixture

mogul-style beef

PREPARATION TIME 15 MINUTES • COOKING TIME 50 MINUTES

1.5kg rump steak
1/4 cup peanut oil (60ml)
3 medium brown onions
(450g), sliced
2 teaspoons garam masala
1/4 teaspoon saffron powder
1 teaspoon ground turmeric
1 teaspoon ground ginger
1/2 teaspoon chilli powder
1/3 cup milk (80ml)
1 tablespoon honey
2/3 cup chicken stock (160ml)
2/3 cup cream (160ml)
2 tablespoons packaged
ground almonds

1 Cut steak into 1.5cm strips.

2 Heat oil in large saucepan; cook onions, stirring, over medium heat for about 3 minutes or until onions are soft. Stir in garam masala, saffron, turmeric, ginger and chilli; cook further minute.

3 Stir in steak, over high heat, until steak is well browned all over. Stir in milk, honey and stock. Bring to a boil, reduce heat; simmer, covered, for about 30 minutes or until steak is tender, stirring occasionally during cooking.

4 Stir in cream and almonds over medium heat, until mixture is heated through.

SERVES 4

per serve 42.8g fat; 3414kJ

tip Curry can be made a day ahead; keep, covered, in refrigerator or freeze for up to 2 months.

Cutting steak into strips

Adding spices to onions

Pouring stock into saucepan

lamb kebabs with curried onions

PREPARATION TIME 30 MINUTES (plus refrigeration time) • COOKING TIME 20 MINUTES

Ask your butcher to bone the lamb for you.

1.5kg leg of lamb, boned
1 medium brown onion
  (150g), chopped
1 teaspoon black poppy seeds
2 teaspoons ground ginger
1/4 teaspoon ground nutmeg
1 teaspoon ground turmeric
1/2 teaspoon garam masala
200g carton plain yogurt

CURRIED ONIONS

30g ghee
2 medium brown onions
  (300g), chopped
1/2 teaspoon paprika
1/2 teaspoon ground cardamom
1/4 teaspoon ground cloves
1/4 teaspoon ground cinnamon
1/2 teaspoon garam masala
1/2 cup water (125ml)

1 Remove excess fat from lamb; cut lamb into 2cm cubes.

2 Blend or process onion, seeds, ginger, nutmeg, turmeric and garam masala until smooth.

3 Combine lamb and onion mixture in medium bowl, stir in yogurt, cover; refrigerate overnight.

4 Thread lamb onto skewers. Barbecue or grill for about 5 minutes or until golden brown and tender. Serve with curried onions and rice.

  curried onions Heat ghee in medium saucepan; cook onions, stirring, over medium heat for about 4 minutes or until onions are soft. Stir in paprika, cardamom, cloves, cinnamon and garam masala over medium heat for 1 minute. Stir in the water over medium heat for 2 minutes or until mixture boils and thickens slightly.

SERVES 4

per serve 16.2g fat; 1911kJ
tip Recipe may be prepared a day ahead; keep, covered, in refrigerator.

Adding onion mixture to lamb

Placing skewers onto grill

Adding spices to onion

poultry

In India, poultry is quite expensive so it is a delicacy reserved for special occasions. In some other Asian countries, however, poultry is so readily available that it is taken for granted. Our recipes are from many regions and have been simplified; although the unique flavours of herb-and-spice combinations remain.

sour duck curry

PREPARATION TIME 15 MINUTES (plus standing time) • COOKING TIME 50 MINUTES

No. 16 duck
1 large brown onion (200g),
   chopped finely
1 tablespoon ground coriander
1 teaspoon ground ginger
1/2 teaspoon ground turmeric
1/2 teaspoon ground cardamom
1/4 teaspoon paprika
1 teaspoon tamarind concentrate
2 cups chicken stock (500ml)
2 tablespoons water
1 tablespoon cornflour
1 tablespoon chopped
   fresh coriander

1 Cut duck into serving-sized pieces. Cook duck, in batches, in large heated pan until browned both sides.

2 Remove from pan; drain on absorbent paper.

3 Drain fat from pan, reserving 1 tablespoon. Heat reserved fat in same pan; cook onion, stirring 1 minute. Add ground coriander, ginger, turmeric, cardamom and paprika; cook, stirring for further 2 minutes or until spices become fragrant. Stir in tamarind and stock.

4 Return duck to pan, bring to boil; simmer, uncovered, 30 minutes or until duck is tender.

5 Combine the water and flour in small bowl; stir into duck mixture. Stir over medium heat until sauce boils and thickens. Stir fresh coriander through just before serving.

SERVES 4

per serve 56.1g fat; 2652kJ
tip Curry is best prepared just before serving.

Cutting duck into serving-sized pieces

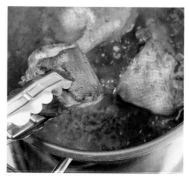
Returning duck to pan

grilled chicken curry with spicy coconut sauce

PREPARATION TIME 10 MINUTES • COOKING TIME 50 MINUTES

2 tablespoons peanut oil
4 chicken marylands (1.4kg)
1 medium brown onion (150g),
  chopped finely
1 clove garlic, crushed
1 tablespoon finely chopped fresh
  lemon grass
2 tablespoons ground coriander
1 tablespoon ground cumin
1 teaspoon ground cardamom
1/2 teaspoon ground cloves
1/2 teaspoon chilli powder
2 x 400ml cans coconut cream
1 tablespoon light soy sauce
1/4 cup chopped fresh coriander

1 Heat oil in large saucepan. Cook chicken over high heat for about 5 minutes or until chicken is browned all over, turning frequently. Remove chicken from pan.

2 Add onion to pan; stir over medium heat for about 3 minutes or until onion is soft. Stir in garlic, lemon grass, ground coriander, cumin, cardamom, cloves and chilli; stir over medium heat for a further minute.

3 Add chicken to pan; turn chicken to coat with spice mixture. Stir in coconut cream and sauce; bring to boil. Reduce heat; cover, simmer for about 15 minutes or until tender.

4 Remove chicken from sauce; cook chicken under hot grill until crisp and browned all over. Boil sauce, uncovered, until reduced by one-third. Stir in fresh coriander; mix well. Serve sauce over chicken.

SERVES 4

per serve 75.2g fat; 3861kJ
tip Curry is best made close to serving time.

Cooking chicken over high heat

Adding spices to onion in pan

Stirring in coconut cream and sauce

chicken peanut curry

PREPARATION TIME 10 MINUTES • COOKING TIME 1 HOUR

We used the red curry paste from the curry blends and pastes section in this book.

8 chicken thigh cutlets (1.3kg)
1/4 cup peanut oil (60ml)
1/3 cup red curry paste (85g)
400ml can coconut milk
1/4 cup fish sauce (60ml)
2 tablespoons sugar
1/2 cup crunchy peanut
**   butter (130g)**

1 Place chicken into baking dish; brush with 1 tablespoon of the oil. Bake in moderately hot oven for about 45 minutes or until chicken is tender; drain on absorbent paper.

2 Heat remaining oil in medium saucepan; cook curry paste. Stir over medium heat for 1 minute.

3 Stir in coconut milk, sauce, sugar and peanut butter, over medium heat, until mixture boils and thickens.

4 Add chicken to coconut mixture; stir over medium heat for about 5 minutes or until mixture is hot.

SERVES 4

per serve 88.8g fat; 4541kJ
tip Curry can be made a day ahead; keep, covered, in refrigerator.

Brushing chicken with oil

Cooking curry paste

green duck curry

PREPARATION TIME 15 MINUTES • COOKING TIME 1 HOUR 25 MINUTES

We used the green masala paste from the curry blends and pastes section in this book.

400ml can coconut cream
2 tablespoons green masala paste
No. 20 duck
400ml can coconut milk
1 cup water (250ml)
8 dried lime leaves
1 tablespoon sugar
1 tablespoon dried basil
3 small fresh red chillies, seeded
3 small fresh green
   chillies, seeded

1 Combine coconut cream and paste in large saucepan; bring to boil. Reduce heat; simmer, uncovered, for about 10 minutes or until mixture is reduced by one-third.

2 Cut duck into eight pieces and add to saucepan; bring to boil. Reduce heat; simmer, uncovered, for 15 minutes, stirring occasionally.

3 Stir in coconut milk, the water and lime leaves; bring to boil. Reduce heat; simmer, uncovered, for about 40 minutes or until duck is tender.

4 Stir in sugar, basil and chillies; simmer further 5 minutes. Sprinkle with flaked coconut, if desired.

SERVES 4

per serve 125g fat; 5345kJ

tip Curry can be made a day ahead; keep, covered, in refrigerator.

Combining coconut cream and paste

Adding duck pieces to pan

chicken and almond curry

PREPARATION TIME 15 MINUTES (plus cooling time) • COOKING TIME 1 HOUR

3 medium brown onions (450g)
1 tablespoon peanut oil
60g ghee
1kg chicken thigh fillets, halved
2 cloves garlic, crushed
2 teaspoons grated fresh ginger
1 teaspoon fennel seeds
1 cinnamon stick
1 tablespoon ground coriander
1 tablespoon ground cumin
1 teaspoon ground turmeric
1/2 teaspoon chilli powder
3 medium tomatoes (570g),
  peeled, chopped
1 tablespoon tomato paste
1 tablespoon peanut oil, extra
3/4 cup blanched almonds (120g)
3/4 cup plain yogurt (180ml)
1/2 cup packaged ground
  almonds (90g)
2 teaspoons garam masala
1/2 cup chopped fresh coriander

1 Slice half of the onions; chop remaining onions. Heat oil and ghee in large saucepan; cook chicken, in batches, over medium heat for about 5 minutes or until chicken is browned all over. Remove chicken from pan.

2 Add sliced onions to pan; stir over medium heat for about 3 minutes (or microwave on HIGH for about 3 minutes) or until onions are soft. Remove onions from pan; reserve.

3 Add chopped onions to pan with garlic and ginger; stir over medium heat for about 3 minutes (or microwave on HIGH for about 3 minutes) or until onions are soft. Stir in seeds, cinnamon stick, ground coriander, cumin, turmeric and chilli; stir over medium heat for 1 minute (or microwave on HIGH for 30 seconds). Stir in tomato and paste; bring to boil. Reduce heat; cover, simmer for 10 minutes (or microwave on MEDIUM for 4 minutes), stirring occasionally.

4 Add chicken to pan; stir to coat chicken. Cover; cook over low heat for about 20 minutes (or microwave on MEDIUM for about 10 minutes) or until chicken is tender.

5 Heat extra oil in small frying pan; cook almonds. Stir over medium heat until almonds are golden brown; drain on absorbent paper. Stir yogurt and toasted almonds into curry; cover, simmer for 5 minutes (or microwave on HIGH for 2 minutes), stirring occasionally. Stir in reserved sliced onions, ground almonds, garam masala and fresh coriander, over medium heat, until heated through.

SERVES 4

per serve 65.8g fat; 3860kJ
tip Curry can be made a day ahead; keep, covered, in refrigerator.

Cooking chicken in batches

Stirring sliced onions in pan

Adding ground coriander to pan

spicy dry chicken curry

PREPARATION TIME 10 MINUTES • COOKING TIME 1 HOUR

60g ghee
10 dried curry leaves, crumbled
1/2 teaspoon black mustard seeds
1 medium brown onion
   (150g), chopped
1 clove garlic, crushed
1 tablespoon grated fresh ginger
2 teaspoons curry powder
1 teaspoon tandoori mix
1 teaspoon ground cumin
1/2 teaspoon garam masala
1 teaspoon chilli powder
1 tablespoon lemon juice
1/4 cup water (60ml)
8 chicken thigh cutlets (1.3kg)

1 Heat ghee in large frying pan; add leaves and seeds. Stir over high heat for about 1 minute or until seeds begin to pop.

2 Stir in onion, garlic and ginger, over medium heat, for about 3 minutes or until onion is soft.

3 Stir in curry powder, tandoori mix, cumin, garam masala and chilli, over medium heat, for further minute; stir in juice and the water.

4 Add chicken to pan; turn chicken to coat evenly with curry mixture. Cover; cook over low heat for about 50 minutes or until chicken is tender, turning chicken occasionally. Add a little extra water, if necessary, during cooking time.

SERVES 4

per serve 45.3g fat; 2451kJ

tip Curry can be prepared a day ahead; keep, covered, in refrigerator or freeze for up to 2 months.

Stirring leaves and seeds with ghee

Adding spices to pan

Turning chicken

spicy fried chicken

PREPARATION TIME 10 MINUTES (plus refrigeration time) • COOKING TIME 20 MINUTES

2 cloves garlic, crushed
1 tablespoon grated fresh ginger
2 teaspoons ground cardamom
1 teaspoon ground nutmeg
1 small fresh red chilli,
   chopped finely
2 tablespoons lemon juice
1.5kg chicken thigh cutlets
15g ghee
1 tablespoon peanut oil
1/2 cup unsalted roasted
   cashew nuts (75g)
1/4 cup water (60ml)

1 Combine garlic, ginger, cardamom, nutmeg, chilli and juice in medium bowl; mix well.

2 Add chicken to marinade; mix well. Cover; refrigerate for several hours or overnight.

3 Heat ghee and oil in large frying pan; add chicken. Cook over medium heat for about 5 minutes or until chicken is lightly browned all over.

4 Stir in nuts, then the water. Cover; simmer for about 10 minutes or until chicken is tender.

SERVES 4

per serve 49.9g fat; 2788kJ

tip Chicken can be prepared a day ahead; cook just before serving.

Combining marinade ingredients

Adding chicken to spice mixture

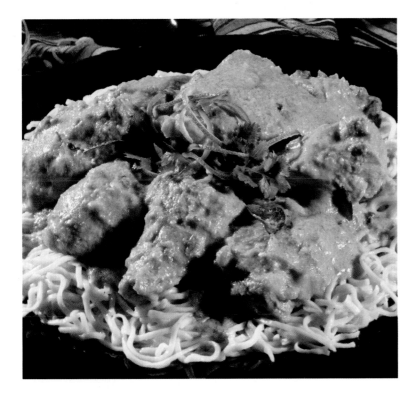

Cutting leg and thigh from chicken

Cutting wing from chicken

mild chicken curry

PREPARATION TIME 20 MINUTES • COOKING TIME 50 MINUTES

No. 15 chicken
4 cloves garlic, crushed
1 large brown onion
   (200g), chopped
2 tablespoons peanut oil
1 tablespoon chopped fresh ginger
1/2 teaspoon shrimp paste
2 teaspoons sambal oelek
1/2 teaspoon ground turmeric
2 teaspoons lime juice
1 teaspoon sesame oil
2 teaspoons peanut oil, extra
6 dried curry leaves
1 cinnamon stick
2 teaspoons chopped dried
   lime rind
400ml can coconut cream
1/2 cup water (125ml)
11/2 tablespoons besan flour
2 tablespoons water, extra

1 Cut legs and thighs from chicken in one piece; cut legs from thighs.

2 Cut wings from chicken with a small amount of breast meat; remove and discard wing tips.

3 Cut breasts from chicken, cutting through rib bones along each side of body; cut close to backbone. Cut breasts into quarters. Trim away any excess fat or skin.

4 Blend or process garlic, onion, peanut oil, ginger, paste, sambal, turmeric and juice until smooth. Heat sesame oil and extra peanut oil in large frying pan; add garlic mixture, curry leaves, cinnamon and rind. Stir over medium heat for 3 minutes (or microwave on HIGH for 4 minutes).

5 Add chicken pieces to pan; cook over medium heat for about 3 minutes, turning once. Stir in coconut cream and the water; bring to boil. Reduce heat; cover, simmer for about 30 minutes (or microwave on HIGH for about 20 minutes) or until chicken is tender, stirring often.

6 Remove chicken from pan; keep warm. Blend flour with the extra water; stir into coconut mixture. Stir over high heat (or microwave on HIGH for about 4 minutes) until mixture boils and thickens. Remove cinnamon stick. Serve sauce over chicken. Serve with egg noodles, if desired.

SERVES 4

per serve 62.1g fat; 3187kJ

tip Curry can be made 3 days ahead; keep, covered, in refrigerator or freeze for up to 2 months.

creamy chicken and basil curry

PREPARATION TIME 15 MINUTES (plus cooling time) • COOKING TIME 40 MINUTES

750g chicken thigh fillets
2 tablespoons peanut oil
1 tablespoon grated galangal
2 x 400ml cans coconut milk
1 tablespoon fish sauce
¹/₄ cup chopped fresh basil leaves

GREEN CURRY PASTE
8 small fresh green chillies
3 cloves garlic
2 stalks fresh lemon grass
3 fresh coriander roots and stems
2 teaspoons grated lime rind
1 teaspoon caraway seeds
1 teaspoon ground turmeric
1 teaspoon shrimp paste
2 tablespoons water

1 Cut chicken into 1cm strips.

2 Heat oil in large saucepan; cook 2 tablespoons green curry paste. Stir over high heat for 1 minute. Add chicken to pan; stir over medium heat for about 3 minutes or until chicken is well coated in curry paste and lightly browned all over.

3 Add galangal. Stir in coconut milk; bring to boil. Reduce heat; simmer, uncovered, for about 45 minutes or until mixture is thick. Stir in fish sauce and basil.

green curry paste Roughly chop chillies, garlic, lemon grass and coriander; blend or process with rind, seeds, turmeric, paste and the water until finely chopped.

SERVES 4

per serve 64.1g fat; 3195kJ

tip Curry paste will keep for 2 weeks in jar in refrigerator. Curry is best made close to serving time.

Cutting chicken into strips

Stirring in coconut milk

Chopping lemon grass

curried chicken with tomatoes and peanuts

PREPARATION TIME 20 MINUTES • COOKING TIME 1 HOUR 5 MINUTES

We used the musaman curry paste from the curry blends and pastes section in this book.

No. 15 chicken
2 tablespoons peanut oil
2 medium brown onions
    (300g), chopped
1 teaspoon sugar
1 teaspoon chopped fresh ginger
1 bay leaf
1 quantity musaman curry paste
400ml can coconut cream
1¹/₂ tablespoons plain flour
2 tablespoons water
2 medium tomatoes
    (380g), chopped
2 teaspoons peanut oil, extra
1 clove garlic, sliced
¹/₄ cup chopped unroasted
    peanuts (35g)

1 Cut legs and thighs from chicken in one piece; cut thighs from legs.

2 Cut wings from chicken with a small amount of breast meat; remove and discard wing tips.

3 Cut breasts from chicken, cutting through rib bones along each side of body; cut close to backbone. Cut breasts into quarters. Trim away excess fat or skin.

4 Heat oil in large frying pan; cook onion, sugar, ginger and bay leaf. Stir over medium heat for about 4 minutes (or microwave on HIGH for about 5 minutes) or until onions are soft. Stir in curry paste over medium heat for about 2 minutes (or microwave on HIGH for about 1 minute) or until fragrant. Add chicken; cook over medium heat until lightly browned. Transfer mixture to large saucepan; add coconut cream. Simmer, covered, for about 30 minutes (or microwave on HIGH for about 20 minutes) or until chicken is tender.

5 Remove chicken from saucepan. Blend flour with the water; stir into coconut mixture. Stir over high heat (or microwave on HIGH for about 3 minutes) or until mixture boils and thickens. Return chicken to pan; add tomato, stir until mixture is hot. Heat extra oil in small frying pan; cook garlic and nuts. Stir over medium heat until nuts are lightly browned; serve sprinkled over chicken.

SERVES 4

per serve 67.3g fat; 3560kJ

tip This dish can be made 3 days ahead; keep, covered, in refrigerator or freeze before the addition of tomato for up to 3 months.

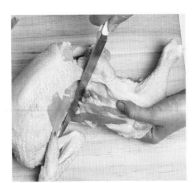
Cutting leg and thigh from chicken

Cutting breast from chicken

Adding flour and water to pan

tandoori chicken

PREPARATION TIME 20 MINUTES • COOKING TIME 1 HOUR 5 MINUTES

2 x No. 9 chickens
200g carton plain yogurt
2 cloves garlic, crushed
2 teaspoons grated fresh ginger
1 tablespoon tandoori mix
60g ghee, melted

1 Using scissors, cut through skin of chickens along breastbone.

2 Using fingers (and scissors where necessary), gently ease all skin from chickens, except from wings. Remove and discard skin.

3 Cut a few slits, about 1cm deep, in chicken breasts and drumsticks.

4 Combine yogurt, garlic, ginger and tandoori mix in small bowl; mix well. Place chickens in baking dish; brush inside and out with yogurt mixture.

5 Drizzle a little ghee over chickens; bake in moderately hot oven for 20 minutes. Turn chickens; bake further 15 minutes. Turn chickens onto one side; bake further 15 minutes. Turn chickens over and bake further 15 minutes or until chickens are well browned and tender. Brush chickens with ghee occasionally during cooking.

SERVES 4

per serve 45.6g fat; 2457kJ

tip We used the tandoori mix from the curry blends and pastes section in this book. Chicken is best cooked close to serving time.

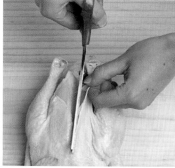
Cutting through chicken skin

Cutting slits in chicken breast

Brushing chicken with yogurt mixture

Pricking chicken with fork

Cooking chicken in batches

marinated chicken curry

PREPARATION TIME 20 MINUTES (plus refrigeration time) • COOKING TIME 45 MINUTES

1kg chicken thigh fillets, halved
1 tablespoon peanut oil
60g ghee
1 medium brown onion
  (150g), chopped
1 tablespoon grated fresh ginger
2 teaspoons cumin seeds
6 medium tomatoes (540g),
  peeled, chopped
1 tablespoon tomato paste
1 teaspoon sugar
1/2 cup sour cream (125ml)
2 teaspoons garam masala
1/2 cup chopped fresh coriander

MARINADE

1/2 cup plain yogurt (125ml)
1/3 cup lime juice (80ml)
1 clove garlic, crushed
1 teaspoon ground cardamom
1 teaspoon ground coriander
1/2 teaspoon ground cinnamon
1/2 teaspoon chilli powder
1/4 teaspoon ground cloves

1 Place chicken in large bowl. Prick chicken all over with fork; add marinade, mix well. Cover; refrigerate for several hours or overnight, stirring occasionally. Drain chicken; reserve remaining marinade.

2 Heat oil and ghee in large saucepan; add chicken in batches. Cook over high heat for about 5 minutes or until browned all over. Remove chicken from pan.

3 Add onion and ginger to same pan; stir over medium heat for about 2 minutes (or microwave on HIGH for about 2 minutes) or until onion is soft. Stir in seeds over medium heat for 1 minute (or microwave on HIGH for 30 seconds). Stir in tomato, paste and sugar; bring to boil. Reduce heat; cover, simmer for about 15 minutes (or microwave on HIGH for about 10 minutes) or until sauce is thick.

4 Stir in chicken, reserved marinade and sour cream; bring to boil. Reduce heat; cover, simmer for about 15 minutes (or microwave on MEDIUM for about 15 minutes) or until chicken is tender, stirring occasionally.

5 Stir in garam masala and coriander; mix well.

marinade Combine ingredients in small bowl; mix well.

SERVES 4

per serve 39.8g fat; 2714kJ
tip Curry can be made 2 days ahead; keep, covered, in refrigerator.

duck vindaloo

PREPARATION TIME 15 MINUTES (plus refrigeration time) • COOKING TIME 40 MINUTES

No. 20 duck
6 small fresh red chillies, seeded
2 cloves garlic, crushed
3/4 cup brown vinegar (180ml)
1 tablespoon chopped fresh ginger
1 teaspoon cumin seeds
1 teaspoon coriander seeds
1/2 teaspoon cardamom seeds
1 teaspoon fenugreek seeds
1 teaspoon ground turmeric
1 tablespoon sugar
45g ghee

1 Cut duck into serving-sized pieces; place into large bowl.

2 Blend or process chillies, garlic, vinegar, ginger, seeds, turmeric and sugar until smooth.

3 Pour mixture over duck; stir well. Cover; refrigerate for several hours or overnight, turning occasionally.

4 Remove duck from mixture; reserve mixture. Heat ghee in large frying pan; add duck to pan. Cook over medium heat for about 5 minutes or until duck is browned all over.

5 Stir in reserved mixture; bring to boil. Reduce heat; cover, simmer for about 30 minutes or until tender.

SERVES 6

per serve 60.1g fat; 2630kJ
tip This dish is best made just before serving.

Cutting duck into pieces

Pouring mixture over duck

Adding reserved mixture to pan

side dishes

Although traditional Indian and Asian cuisines do not include Western-style salads, an array of contrasting tastes and textures is introduced into a meal by the side dishes served. These chutneys, sambals and salads are intended to stimulate your tastebuds and appetite, and should be made in small quantities because they are served only in small amounts. The side dishes made from fresh ingredients do not keep for more than a day.

spicy date chutney

PREPARATION TIME 10 MINUTES
(plus standing time)

6 cups seeded dried dates (1kg)
1 litre water (4 cups)
1 tablespoon grated fresh ginger
3 fresh green chillies, chopped
1/4 cup lime juice (60ml)
1 clove garlic, crushed
1 tablespoon ground coriander
1 tablespoon ground cumin
1 teaspoon chilli powder

1 Combine dates and the water in large bowl, cover; stand for 2 hours.

2 Drain dates, reserve 3/4 cup of the liquid. Blend or process dates, remaining ingredients and reserved liquid until smooth. Spoon chutney into jars; seal.

MAKES ABOUT 4 CUPS

per 100g 0.3g fat; 554kJ

tip Chutney can be made 1 month ahead; store, covered, in refrigerator.

fresh coriander and coconut chutney

PREPARATION TIME 10 MINUTES

1/3 cup boiling water (80ml)
1/3 cup shredded coconut (25g)
2 cups loosely packed fresh coriander leaves
4 cloves garlic, chopped
1 small brown onion (80g), chopped
1 1/2 teaspoons garam masala
1/4 cup lemon juice (60ml)
2 tablespoons lime juice
1 small fresh red chilli, chopped

1 Pour the water over coconut in small bowl, cover; stand for about 5 minutes or until liquid is absorbed.

2 Blend or process coconut mixture, coriander, garlic, onion, garam masala and juices until well combined. Return mixture to bowl, stir in chilli.

MAKES ABOUT 1 1/2 CUPS

per 100g 4.8g fat; 269kJ

tip Chutney can be made a day ahead; store, covered, in refrigerator.

FRESH CORIANDER AND COCONUT CHUTNEY

SPICY DATE CHUTNEY

tamarind sambal

PREPARATION TIME 10 MINUTES

1 tablespoon tamarind concentrate
2 tablespoons water
1 teaspoon ground cumin
1/2 teaspoon chilli powder
1/2 teaspoon ground fennel
1 1/2 tablespoons palm sugar
2 teaspoons grated fresh ginger
1 tablespoon lemon juice

1 Combine tamarind and the water in small bowl; stir until dissolved.

2 Stir cumin, chilli and fennel into tamarind mixture.

3 Stir in palm sugar, ginger and juice, stir until sugar is dissolved.

MAKES ABOUT 1/2 CUP

per 1/2 cup 1g fat; 756kJ

tip Sambal can be made a day ahead; store, covered, in refrigerator.

TAMARIND SAMBAL

hot tomato chutney

PREPARATION TIME 10 MINUTES
COOKING TIME 15 MINUTES

Serve chutney hot or cold with curries, rice, vegetables or breads.

1 tablespoon oil
1/2 teaspoon black mustard seeds
2 cloves garlic, chopped
1 small fresh red chilli, chopped finely
1 teaspoon chopped fresh ginger
1 cinnamon stick
1 teaspoon ground cumin
1 teaspoon ground turmeric
410g can tomatoes
1 teaspoon brown sugar
6 dried curry leaves

1 Heat oil in small saucepan, stir in seeds, cover; cook over medium heat until seeds begin to pop. Stir in garlic, chilli, ginger and cinnamon; stir over medium heat for about 3 minutes or until garlic is golden brown.

2 Stir in cumin and turmeric; stir over medium heat for 2 minutes. Stir in undrained crushed tomatoes, sugar and curry leaves, bring to boil; reduce heat, simmer, uncovered, for about 5 minutes or until chutney is thick. Discard cinnamon, pour chutney into jar; seal when cold.

MAKES ABOUT 1 CUP

per 100g 4.8g fat; 270kJ

tip Chutney can be made a week ahead; store, covered, in refrigerator.

HOT TOMATO CHUTNEY

seafood

Plentiful, fresh seafood is an important part of the flourishing cuisine of Indian coastal communities. Other regions of this sprawling country boast an abundance of freshwater fish, and dried prawns, available in packets, are eaten all over India and Pakistan. Fresh seafood also features prominently in the diets of the people of South-East Asia, and preserved fish is considered a delicacy.

curried mussels with mushrooms

PREPARATION TIME 35 MINUTES (plus standing time) • COOKING TIME 25 MINUTES

90 large mussels (3kg)
1 cup water (250ml)
15g ghee
2 Thai red chillies, chopped finely
1 tablespoon grated fresh ginger
2 cloves garlic, crushed
1 tablespoon chopped fresh
  lemon grass
150g button mushrooms, sliced
400ml can coconut milk
1 tablespoon fish sauce
1 tablespoon brown sugar
4 green onions, chopped
2 teaspoons plain flour
1 tablespoon water, extra
1 tablespoon chopped fresh
  basil leaves

1 Scrub mussels under cold running water; remove beards. Combine mussels and the water in large saucepan, cover; bring to boil. Reduce heat; simmer for 2 minutes, stirring occasionally. Drain mussels.

2 Heat ghee in large frying pan or wok; add chilli, ginger, garlic, lemon grass and mushrooms, stirring, over medium heat for about 2 minutes.

3 Stir in coconut milk, sauce and sugar; bring to boil. Reduce heat; simmer, uncovered, for 1 minute. Stir in onion; cook over medium heat for 1 minute. Blend flour with the extra water, stir into mushroom mixture; stir over high heat until sauce boils and thickens.

4 Stir in mussels and basil; stir over medium heat until heated through.

SERVES 4

per serve 30.3g fat; 1807kJ
tip Recipe is best made just before serving.

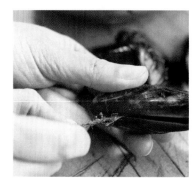
Removing beard from mussel

Adding coconut milk to pan

curried prawns with lemon and tomato

PREPARATION TIME 20 MINUTES (plus refrigeration time) • COOKING TIME 20 MINUTES

20 large uncooked prawns (1kg)
1/4 cup lemon juice (60ml)
1/4 cup cider vinegar (60ml)
15g ghee
1 tablespoon peanut oil
2 cloves garlic, crushed
1 medium brown onion
   (150g), chopped
1 teaspoon ground cumin
1/2 teaspoon ground turmeric
1/4 teaspoon chilli powder
1 teaspoon black mustard seeds
1 tablespoon grated fresh ginger
1 teaspoon brown sugar
1 tablespoon tomato paste
2 teaspoons plain flour
1/4 cup water (60ml)
400g can tomatoes

1 Shell and devein prawns, leaving tails intact.

2 Combine prawns, juice and vinegar in medium bowl. Cover; refrigerate for 30 minutes.

3 Heat ghee and oil in medium saucepan; add garlic and onion. Stir over medium heat for about 2 minutes, or until onion is soft.

4 Stir in cumin, turmeric, chilli, seeds, ginger and sugar. Stir over medium heat for about 1 minute, or until seeds begin to pop.

5 Add paste, then blended flour and water. Stir in undrained crushed tomatoes; bring to boil. Reduce heat; simmer, uncovered, for about 10 minutes or until mixture thickens slightly.

6 Add prawn mixture; stir over medium heat for about 4 minutes, or until prawns are tender.

SERVES 4

per serve 9.8g fat; 1053kJ

tip Recipe can be made a day ahead; store, covered, in refrigerator.

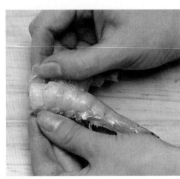
Shelling prawns

Combining juice and vinegar with prawns

Adding prawn mixture to pan

Pulling crab shell away from body

Adding garam masala to pan

gingered crab curry

PREPARATION TIME 20 MINUTES • COOKING TIME 50 MINUTES

We used the Kashmiri-style garam masala from the curry blends and pastes section in this book.

**4 medium uncooked blue
swimmer crabs (3kg)**
¹/₄ cup peanut oil (60ml)
**2 large brown onions
(400g), chopped**
3 cloves garlic, crushed
2 teaspoons grated fresh ginger
2 bay leaves
1 teaspoon coriander seeds
2 small fresh red chillies, chopped
1 tablespoon garam masala
2 tablespoons poppy seeds
**2 tablespoons packaged
ground almonds**
**¹/₄ cup chopped fresh
coriander leaves**
425g can tomato puree
1¹/₂ cups coconut cream (375ml)

1 Gently pull crab shell away from body. Rinse under cold water; drain. Repeat with remaining crabs.

2 Heat oil in large frying pan; add onion, garlic, ginger, bay leaves, coriander seeds, chilli and garam masala. Stir over heat for about 3 minutes, or until onions are soft.

3 Stir in poppy seeds, almond, fresh coriander and tomato puree, bring to boil; stir in coconut cream. Reduce heat; simmer, uncovered, for 5 minutes.

4 Add crabs to sauce; cover, simmer for 20 minutes. Turn crabs, cover; simmer for further 15 minutes or until crabs are cooked through. Serve with boiled rice, if desired.

SERVES 4

per serve 40.1g fat; 2644kJ

tip Recipe is best prepared close to serving time.

mustard prawn curry

PREPARATION TIME 20 MINUTES (plus standing time) • COOKING TIME 20 MINUTES

1kg uncooked king prawns
4 small dried red chillies
1 tablespoon black mustard seeds
30g ghee
2 tablespoons peanut oil
3 medium brown onions
(450g), grated
2 cloves garlic, crushed
2 teaspoons cumin seeds
1/2 teaspoon ground turmeric
1 tablespoon brown sugar
1 cup water (250ml)
1 tablespoon lemon juice
8 dried curry leaves

1 Shell and devein prawns, leaving tails intact.

2 Combine chillies and mustard seeds in small bowl; cover with boiling water. Stand for 10 minutes; drain.

3 Heat ghee and oil in medium saucepan; add onion and garlic. Stir over medium heat for about 2 minutes, or until onion is soft. Stir in mustard seed mixture, cumin seeds, turmeric, sugar, the water and juice; bring to boil. Reduce heat; simmer, uncovered, for about 10 minutes or until mixture has thickened slightly.

4 Blend or process mixture until smooth. Return mixture to saucepan.

5 Stir in curry leaves and prawns; stir over medium heat for about 4 minutes, or until prawns are tender.

SERVES 6

per serve 12.2g fat; 889kJ
tip Recipe is best made just before serving.

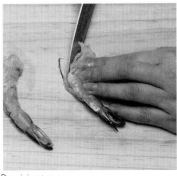

Deveining prawns

Adding seeds, sugar and turmeric to pan

fish cutlets with tamarind and coconut

PREPARATION TIME 10 MINUTES (plus standing and cooling time) • COOKING TIME 25 MINUTES

We used jewfish cutlets in this recipe.

2 tablespoons desiccated coconut
1 tablespoon coriander seeds
2 teaspoons cumin seeds
1 red Thai chilli, seeded,
  chopped finely
2 cloves garlic, crushed
1 teaspoon grated fresh ginger
2 tablespoons tamarind sauce
15g ghee
1 medium brown onion
  (150g), chopped
1¹/₂ cups coconut cream (375ml)
4 white fish cutlets (1kg)

1 Stir coconut in small frying pan over medium heat until lightly browned; remove from pan. Add seeds to pan; stir over medium heat for about 2 minutes or until lightly browned. Remove from pan; cool.

2 Blend or process coconut, seeds, chilli, garlic, ginger and sauce until smooth and pasty.

3 Heat ghee in medium frying pan, add onion; stir over medium heat for about 2 minutes or until onion is soft. Stir in coconut mixture; stir over medium heat for 1 minute.

4 Stir in coconut cream, bring to boil; reduce heat. Add cutlets; simmer, uncovered, for about 8 minutes or until cutlets are tender. Turn cutlets halfway through cooking time.

SERVES 4

per serve 31g fat; 2010kJ
tip Paste can be made a day ahead; store, covered, in refrigerator.

Stirring seeds over medium heat

Stirring ghee, onion and coconut mixture

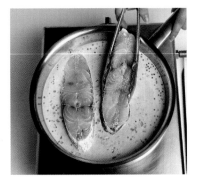
Adding cutlets to pan

Removing heads and legs of prawns

Placing prawns on grill

marinated grilled prawns

PREPARATION TIME 20 MINUTES (plus refrigeration time) • COOKING TIME 10 MINUTES

Prawn shells are usually eaten in this recipe but shells can be removed before adding prawns to marinade, if preferred.

20 large uncooked prawns (1kg)
1 medium brown onion
(150g), chopped
1/2 cup plain yogurt (125ml)
1/2 teaspoon ground turmeric
1/2 teaspoon chilli powder
1 tablespoon paprika
1 teaspoon grated fresh ginger
2 cloves garlic, crushed
1 tablespoon lemon juice

1 Wash prawns; pat dry with absorbent paper. Remove heads and legs, leaving tails and body shells intact.

2 Blend or process onion, yogurt, turmeric, chilli, paprika, ginger, garlic and juice until smooth. Combine yogurt mixture and prawns in large bowl; mix well. Cover; refrigerate overnight.

3 Grill or barbecue prawns until tender, brushing occasionally with marinade during cooking.

SERVES 4

per serve 2.3g fat; 640kJ

curried octopus with tomatoes and tamarind

PREPARATION TIME 20 MINUTES (plus standing time) • COOKING TIME 25 MINUTES

2 teaspoons tamarind pulp
3/4 cup boiling water (180ml)
1kg baby octopus
30g ghee
1 medium brown onion
   (150g), chopped
2 cloves garlic, crushed
2 teaspoons grated fresh ginger
1 cinnamon stick
2 teaspoons ground cumin
1/2 teaspoon ground turmeric
1/4 teaspoon chilli powder
2 teaspoons ground coriander
400g can tomatoes, drained
1 tablespoon tomato paste
3/4 cup coconut cream (180ml)

1 Combine tamarind pulp and the water in small bowl; cover, stand for 10 minutes. Drain; reserve liquid. Remove and discard heads and beaks from octopus. Cut octopus tentacles into four.

2 Melt ghee in medium saucepan; add onion, garlic and ginger. Stir over medium heat for about 3 minutes (or microwave on HIGH for 4 minutes) or until onion is soft.

3 Add cinnamon, cumin, turmeric, chilli and coriander; stir over medium heat for 2 minutes (or microwave on HIGH for 1 minute).

4 Stir in reserved tamarind liquid, crushed tomatoes, paste and coconut cream; bring to boil. Reduce heat; simmer, covered, for 10 minutes (or microwave on HIGH for 10 minutes), stirring occasionally.

5 Stir in octopus; simmer, covered, for about 3 minutes (or microwave on HIGH for about 2 minutes), or until octopus is tender. Serve with rice, if desired.

SERVES 4

per serve 18.8g fat; 1287kJ

tip Sauce can be made several hours ahead; add octopus just before serving. Store sauce, covered, in refrigerator.

Removing head and beak from octopus

Stirring octopus into pan

masala prawns

PREPARATION TIME 20 MINUTES (plus marinating time) • COOKING TIME 10 MINUTES

750g uncooked king prawns
2 teaspoons grated fresh ginger
3 cloves garlic, chopped
1 teaspoon chilli powder
1/2 teaspoon garam masala
1/2 teaspoon ground cinnamon
1 teaspoon cumin seeds
1 teaspoon coriander seeds
1 tablespoon tomato paste
1/4 cup brown vinegar (60ml)
1/3 cup peanut oil (80ml)
1 tablespoon vegetable oil
2 large brown onions
  (400g), sliced
1 medium green capsicum
  (200g), sliced

1 Shell and devein prawns, leaving heads and tails intact. Place prawns in large bowl.

2 Blend or process ginger, garlic, chilli, garam masala, cinnamon, seeds and paste until smooth. With motor operating, pour in vinegar and peanut oil in a thin stream.

3 Pour marinade over prawns; mix well. Cover; refrigerate several hours or overnight, stirring occasionally.

4 Heat vegetable oil in large frying pan; stir in onion and capsicum. Stir over medium heat for about 3 minutes (or microwave on HIGH for about 4 minutes) or until onions are soft. Stir in prawn mixture; stir over high heat for about 3 minutes (or microwave on HIGH for about 3 minutes) or until prawns are tender.

SERVES 6

per serve 16.5g fat; 942kJ

tip Recipe can be prepared several hours ahead; cook just before serving.

Adding marinade ingredients to blender

Combining prawns and marinade

Stirring ingredients over high heat

fish curry with lemon grass

PREPARATION TIME 15 MINUTES • COOKING TIME 25 MINUTES

We used ocean perch in this recipe.

1kg boneless fish fillets
1/4 cup peanut oil (60ml)
3 large brown onions
  (600g), sliced
4 cloves garlic, crushed
2 tablespoons chopped
  fresh ginger
1 teaspoon ground turmeric
1 tablespoon chopped fresh
  lemon grass
2 tablespoons brown vinegar
1 tablespoon fish sauce
1/2 cup water (125ml)
2 medium tomatoes
  (380g), chopped
2 tablespoons chopped fresh
  coriander leaves

1 Cut fish into strips. Heat oil in large frying pan; add fish. Stir over medium heat for a few minutes, or until fish is firm. Remove from heat; keep warm.

2 Add onions and garlic to same pan; stir over medium heat for about 5 minutes or until onions are soft.

3 Stir in ginger, turmeric, lemon grass, vinegar and sauce; bring to boil. Reduce heat; simmer, uncovered, for 3 minutes.

4 Stir in fish and the water; bring to boil. Reduce heat; simmer, uncovered, for about 5 minutes, or until fish is tender. Stir in tomato; cook over low heat until mixture is heated through. Serve sprinkled with coriander.

SERVES 4

per serve 21.7g fat; 1918kJ
tip Curry is best made just before serving.

Stirring fish in pan

Adding vinegar and fish sauce to pan

Stirring in fish and the water

vegetables

Spices and delicate flavourings give out-of-the-ordinary appeal to familiar vegetables in this delicious selection of dishes. Some are served hot, some cold, and all can be served at a curry party or as accompaniments to any curry. Most can also be served as main courses on their own.

spicy potato salad

PREPARATION TIME 10 MINUTES • COOKING TIME 30 MINUTES

6 medium potatoes (1.2kg), chopped
1/4 cup peanut oil (60ml)
1 teaspoon black mustard seeds
1 teaspoon cumin seeds
1 teaspoon ground cumin
1/2 teaspoon sweet paprika
11/2 teaspoons turmeric
1/4 teaspoon chilli flakes
1 clove garlic, crushed
2 tablespoons lemon juice
1/4 cup chopped fresh coriander

1 Preheat oven to hot. Boil, steam or microwave potato until just tender, rinse under cold water; drain, cool.

2 Combine potato, oil, seeds, spices, garlic and juice in baking dish. Cook in hot oven about 20 minutes or until potato is brown. Top with coriander to serve.

SERVES 6

per serve 10.2g fat; 960kJ

tip Recipe can be made 3 hours ahead; store, covered, in refrigerator.

savoury chickpeas

PREPARATION TIME 15 MINUTES (plus standing time) • COOKING TIME 1 HOUR 10 MINUTES

1 cup dried chickpeas (200g)
30g ghee
2 medium brown onions
   (300g), chopped
2 cloves garlic, crushed
2 teaspoons grated fresh ginger
1/2 teaspoon ground turmeric
1 teaspoon garam masala
3 cups water (750ml)
2 medium tomatoes (380g),
   peeled, chopped
1 small fresh green chilli,
   seeded, chopped
2 bay leaves
2 tablespoons chopped
   fresh coriander
1 tablespoon lemon juice

1 Place chickpeas in large bowl, cover with water, cover; stand overnight. Rinse and drain chickpeas.

2 Heat ghee in large saucepan, add onion, garlic and ginger; stir over medium heat for about 3 minutes (or microwave on HIGH for about 4 minutes) or until onions are soft. Stir in turmeric and garam masala; stir over medium heat for 1 minute (or microwave on HIGH for 1 minute).

3 Stir in the water, tomato, chilli, bay leaves, half the coriander and all the chickpeas. Bring to boil; reduce heat, cover, simmer for about 1 hour (or microwave on HIGH for about 30 minutes) or until chickpeas are tender, stirring occasionally.

4 Stir in remaining coriander and lemon juice.

SERVES 6

per serve 7.2g fat; 665kJ
tip Recipe is best made just before serving.

Covering chickpeas with water

Adding garam masala to pan

Stirring in the chickpeas

Adding mung beans, onion and ginger

Adding water to vegetables in pan

peppery beans with coconut

PREPARATION TIME 15 MINUTES • COOKING TIME 10 MINUTES

40g ghee
1 teaspoon black mustard seeds
2 tablespoons peeled
  split mung beans
1 small brown onion
  (80g), chopped
1 teaspoon finely chopped
  fresh ginger
1/2 teaspoon cayenne pepper
500g green beans
1 medium red capsicum
  (200g), sliced
1/2 cup water (125ml)
11/2 tablespoons lemon juice
1/2 cup desiccated coconut (45g)

1 Melt ghee in large frying pan, add seeds; stir over medium heat for about 2 minutes or until seeds begin to pop.

2 Stir in mung beans, onion and ginger; stir over medium heat for about 2 minutes or until onion is soft.

3 Stir in cayenne, beans, capsicum and the water; stir over medium heat for about 3 minutes or until beans are tender.

4 Stir in juice, over high heat, for about 1 minute or until heated through. Serve sprinkled with coconut.

SERVES 4

per serve 18g fat; 958kJ

tip Recipe can be made a day ahead; store, covered, in refrigerator.

vegetable curry with coconut cream

PREPARATION TIME 20 MINUTES • COOKING TIME 25 MINUTES

30g ghee
2 medium tomatoes (380g),
   peeled, chopped
3/4 cup coconut cream (180ml)
2 tablespoons plain yogurt
1 medium carrot (120g), sliced
100g green beans,
   chopped into 3cm slices
150g cauliflower, chopped
150g broccoli, chopped
150g button mushrooms, sliced
10 baby eggplants
   (600g), sliced
1/2 cup chopped unsalted
   roasted cashews (75g)

PASTE
1 medium brown onion
   (150g), chopped
1/4 cup desiccated coconut (20g)
3 cloves garlic, chopped
2 teaspoons coriander seeds
2 teaspoons grated fresh ginger
1 teaspoon cumin seeds
1 teaspoon black mustard seeds
1 teaspoon crushed
   dried chillies
1 cinnamon stick
1 1/2 tablespoons water
1/4 teaspoon cardamom seeds
2 cloves

1 Melt ghee in large saucepan, add paste; stir over medium heat for 2 minutes.

2 Stir in tomato, coconut cream and yogurt, bring to boil; reduce heat, simmer, covered, for about 10 minutes.

3 Stir carrot and beans into tomato mixture; stir over medium heat for 3 minutes. Stir in cauliflower, broccoli, mushrooms and eggplant; stir over medium heat for about 4 minutes or until vegetables are just tender.

4 Stir in nuts; mix well.

paste Blend or process ingredients until smooth.

SERVES 4

per serve 31.22g fat; 1698kJ
tip Recipe is best made close to serving time.

Stirring nuts into vegetable curry

spicy silverbeet with yogurt

PREPARATION TIME 10 MINUTES (plus cooling time)
COOKING TIME 10 MINUTES

20 trimmed silverbeet leaves (1.6kg)
40g ghee
2 teaspoons black mustard seeds
1/2 teaspoon fenugreek seeds
1/2 teaspoon ground cumin
1/2 teaspoon ground nutmeg
1/4 teaspoon chilli powder
1 tablespoon brown sugar
400g plain yogurt
1 birdseye chilli, seeded, chopped finely

1 Steam or microwave silverbeet until limp; drain, cool, chop finely.

2 Melt ghee in medium saucepan, stir in seeds, cumin, nutmeg, chilli powder and sugar. Stir over medium heat for about 2 minutes or until mustard seeds begin to pop.

3 Stir in yogurt and silverbeet. Stir over low heat for about 1 minute or until heated through; do not allow mixture to boil. Sprinkle with chilli.

SERVES 4

per serve 12.8g fat; 946kJ

tip Recipe is best made just before serving.

Trimming silverbeet leaves from stalks

Adding silverbeet to saucepan

chickpea and potato salad

PREPARATION TIME 10 MINUTES (plus standing and cooling time) • COOKING TIME 1 HOUR 5 MINUTES

1 cup dried chickpeas (200g)
1 large potato (300g)
2 tablespoons peanut oil
1 clove garlic, crushed
2 teaspoons ground cumin
1 large tomato (250g), chopped
2 small fresh green
**   chillies, chopped**
2 tablespoons chopped
**   fresh coriander**
2 tablespoons lime or lemon juice
1 teaspoon sugar

1　Cover chickpeas with water in large bowl, cover; stand overnight.

2　Drain chickpeas, add to large saucepan of boiling water; boil rapidly, uncovered, for about 1 hour (or microwave on HIGH for about 30 minutes) or until chickpeas are tender. Drain chickpeas; rinse under cold water, drain.

3　Cut potato into 1cm cubes. Heat oil in large frying pan, add potato, garlic and cumin; stir over medium heat for about 5 minutes or until potato is tender. Remove from heat; cool to room temperature.

4　Combine chickpeas, potato, tomato, chilli, coriander, juice and sugar in large bowl; toss gently.

SERVES 6

per serve 8.5g fat; 796kJ

tip Salad can be made a day ahead; store, covered, in refrigerator.

Adding chickpeas to boiling water

Cooking potato and spices

Combining salad ingredients in bowl

Combining ingredients in saucepan

Adding spices and seeds

spicy vegetable dhal

PREPARATION TIME 15 MINUTES • COOKING TIME 50 MINUTES

1 cup red lentils (200g)
1 teaspoon chopped fresh ginger
1 clove garlic, crushed
1 small fresh red chilli,
  chopped finely
1 stick trimmed celery
  (75g), chopped
2 tablespoons chopped
  fresh coriander
1 tablespoon lemon juice
1.25 litres water (5 cups)
2 teaspoons tamarind sauce
3 green onions, chopped
1 medium carrot (120g), chopped
1/2 teaspoon garam masala
1/4 teaspoon ground turmeric
1/4 teaspoon ground coriander
1 teaspoon cumin seeds

1 Wash lentils in cold water; drain well. Combine lentils, ginger, garlic, chilli, celery, fresh coriander, juice, the water, sauce, onion and carrot in medium saucepan. Stir over high heat until mixture boils; reduce heat, simmer, partly covered, for about 40 minutes (or microwave on HIGH for about 25 minutes) or until lentils and vegetables are soft.

2 Blend or process mixture until smooth, return mixture to saucepan. Combine garam masala, turmeric, ground coriander and seeds in small saucepan; stir over medium heat for about 2 minutes (or microwave on HIGH for about 1 minute) or until mixture is fragrant.

3 Add spices and seeds to dhal, mix well. If dhal mixture is too thin, cook over medium heat until thickened (or microwave on HIGH for about 5 minutes). Serve as a sambal with curries.

SERVES 6

per serve 0.9g fat; 430kJ

tip Dhal can be made 3 days ahead; store, covered, in refrigerator or freeze for up to 2 months.

potato and pea curry with yogurt

PREPARATION TIME 15 MINUTES • COOKING TIME 20 MINUTES

1/4 cup vegetable oil (60ml)
1 medium brown onion (150g), chopped finely
2 cloves garlic, crushed
1 teaspoon ground cumin
1/2 teaspoon ground coriander
1/2 teaspoon ground fennel
1/2 teaspoon ground turmeric
1/4 teaspoon cayenne pepper
1 teaspoon garam masala
4 medium potatoes (800g), peeled, chopped
425g can tomatoes
1/2 cup water (125ml)
1 cup frozen peas (125g)

PARSLEY YOGURT
1/2 cup plain yogurt (125ml)
1 tablespoon chopped fresh parsley

1 Heat oil in large pan; cook onion and garlic, stirring, until onion
   is soft. Add spices and potato; cook 2 minutes.

2 Stir in undrained crushed tomatoes and the water, bring to boil; simmer,
   stirring occasionally, about 20 minutes or until potato is tender.

3 Stir in peas; cook, stirring, about 3 minutes or until peas are
   heated through.

   parsley yogurt Combine ingredients in small bowl; mix well.

   SERVES 4

   per serve 16.2g fat; 1288kJ

   tip Parsley yogurt can be made 2 days head. Curry can be made a day
   ahead; store, covered, in refrigerator.

fried eggplants with onions

PREPARATION TIME 10 MINUTES • COOKING TIME 25 MINUTES

2 large eggplants (1kg),
  sliced thinly
vegetable oil for deep-frying
2 tablespoons peanut oil
2 large brown onions
  (400g), sliced
1 teaspoon yellow mustard seeds
1 teaspoon black mustard seeds
2 tablespoons sesame seeds
1/3 cup sultanas (55g)
1/3 cup chopped salted roasted
  cashews (50g)
1/2 teaspoon chilli powder
1 teaspoon ground turmeric
2 teaspoons besan flour
2 teaspoons sugar
2 tablespoons lemon juice
1/3 cup plain yogurt (80ml)
2 tablespoons coconut milk

1 Deep-fry eggplant slices, in batches, in hot vegetable oil for about 2 minutes or until lightly browned; drain on absorbent paper, keep warm.

2 Heat peanut oil in a medium saucepan, add onion and mustard seeds; stir over medium heat for about 4 minutes or until onions are soft and seeds begin to pop. Stir in sesame seeds; stir over medium heat for about 1 minute or until seeds are golden.

3 Stir in sultanas, nuts, chilli, turmeric, flour and sugar; stir over medium heat for 2 minutes.

4 Stir in juice, yogurt and coconut milk, bring to boil; reduce heat, simmer, uncovered, for 3 minutes. Serve onion mixture with eggplants.

SERVES 4

per serve 33g fat; 1897kJ

tip Recipe is best prepared close to serving time.

Deep-frying eggplant slices in batches

Adding sesame seeds to pan

Adding yogurt to pan

tomato, mint and lime salad

PREPARATION TIME 10 MINUTES

4 medium tomatoes (760g)
6 green onions, chopped
1/2 cup chopped fresh mint
1/4 cup lime juice (60ml)
2 teaspoons sugar
1/4 teaspoon chilli powder

1 Cut tomatoes into wedges, combine in large bowl with onion and mint; stir gently.

2 Combine juice, sugar and chilli in small jug, stir into tomato mixture.

SERVES 6

per serve 0.2g fat; 118kJ

tip Salad is best made just before serving.

yogurt with cucumbers

PREPARATION TIME 10 MINUTES
(plus standing time)
COOKING TIME 3 MINUTES

2 small green cucumbers (260g),
 peeled, seeded, chopped finely
coarse cooking salt
2 teaspoons cumin seeds
2 green onions, chopped
1¹/₂ cups plain yogurt (375ml)
1 tablespoon lemon juice

1 Place cucumber in strainer,
 sprinkle with salt; stand for
 15 minutes. Rinse cucumber
 under cold water; drain well.

2 Place seeds in small saucepan,
 stir over low heat until
 well browned.

3 Combine half the cucumber,
 seeds, onion, yogurt and juice
 in medium bowl, stir well. Spoon
 into serving bowl, sprinkle with
 remaining cucumber and extra
 seeds, if desired.

SERVES 6

per serve 2.3g fat; 219kJ

tip Recipe can be made
a day ahead; store covered,
in refrigerator.

Seeding a cucumber

Sprinkling salt over chopped cucumber

Combining cucumber with other ingredients

rice and breads

As rice is served with almost every meal throughout India and Asia, the people of these regions have created a variety of ways of cooking it. For entertaining, they usually choose to serve more interesting rice dishes. Some are cooked in stock with vegetables or lentils, while others are fried with spices, herbs and sometimes meat. The most common breads eaten throughout India are chapati, paratha, roti and puri, which are cooked daily in most households. Naan, another popular bread, is not usually made in the home, as it should be made in a tandoor or clay oven. However, we have modified recipes so that they can all be cooked in today's kitchen.

coconut pilaf

PREPARATION TIME 10 MINUTES • COOKING TIME 35 MINUTES

60g ghee
2 medium brown onions (300g), sliced
1 teaspoon cumin seeds
1 cinnamon stick
4 cardamom pods, bruised
3 whole cloves
1 teaspoon turmeric
1 cup basmati rice (200g)
400ml can coconut cream
1/2 cup water (125ml)
1/2 cup pistachios (75g), toasted, chopped coarsely
1/4 cup currants (35g)

1 Melt ghee in large frying pan; add onion. Stir over medium heat for about 4 minutes or until onion is soft. Stir in seeds, cinnamon, cardamom, cloves and turmeric; stir over medium heat for 2 minutes.

2 Stir in rice; stir over heat for a further minute. Stir in coconut cream and the water, bring to boil. Simmer, covered, about 20 minutes or until all liquid is absorbed and rice is tender. Remove and discard cinnamon stick. Stir through nuts and currants. Stir pilaf with fork before serving.

SERVES 4

per serve 45.3g fat; 2757kJ

tip Pilaf is best made close to serving time.

Adding cumin seeds to pan

Stirring coconut cream into mixture

rice and peas

PREPARATION TIME 10 MINUTES (plus standing time) • COOKING TIME 25 MINUTES

1¹/₂ cups long-grain rice (300g)
15g ghee
4 whole cloves
1 cinnamon stick
4 cardamom pods, bruised
1 teaspoon cumin seeds
¹/₂ teaspoon ground turmeric
¹/₂ cup fresh or frozen peas (60g)
3¹/₂ cups beef stock (875ml)

1 Place rice in medium bowl; cover with cold water. Stand for 30 minutes; drain. Heat ghee in large saucepan; add cloves, cinnamon, cardamom and seeds. Stir over high heat for 1 minute. Stir in turmeric; stir over high heat for 3 minutes.

2 Stir in peas, stock and rice; bring to boil. Reduce heat; cover, simmer for about 15 minutes or until all liquid is absorbed and rice is tender. Remove and discard cinnamon, cloves and cardamom before serving.

SERVES 6

per serve 3g fat; 870kJ
tip Recipe can be made a day ahead; store, covered, in refrigerator.

Adding turmeric to pan

Adding rice to mixture

basic rice

There are several ways to cook rice successfully. It can be boiled, cooked by the absorption method, microwaved, or cooked in a rice cooker following the manufacturer's instructions.

If cooking rice in advance, rinse the cooked rice under cold water until it is cold; drain well. Spread it out on a flat tray covered with absorbent paper or cloth, leave it to dry; store in refrigerator. Rice can be frozen in airtight bags or containers for several months without spoiling.

Rice can be reheated, covered, in a strainer over boiling water. Rice can also be reheated in a microwave oven. Place frozen rice in a dish; cover loosely. Reheat on HIGH.

boiled rice

PREPARATION TIME 5 MINUTES
COOKING TIME 10 MINUTES

1 cup long-grain rice (200g)
1.5 litres water (6 cups)

Place rice in strainer; wash under cold water, drain. Add rice, gradually, to large saucepan of boiling water. Boil, uncovered, for about 10 minutes or until tender; stirring occasionally. Drain rice; stir with fork to separate grains.

SERVES 4

per serve 0.1g fat; 261kJ
tip Rice can be cooked a day ahead; store, covered, in refrigerator.

absorption method

The absorption method of cooking rice is easy, and traditional in Asian countries. Place rice in heavy-based saucepan; add enough cold water to cover the rice and be about 2cm above the surface of the rice. Cover the pan with tight-fitting lid; bring to boil over high heat. Reduce heat to as low as possible; keep covered. Cook for about 20 minutes; remove from heat. Leave covered for a few more minutes to be sure all the water has been completely absorbed by the rice.

microwaved rice

White rice, as a rule, needs double the amount of water to rice; 1 cup white rice takes about 15 minutes to cook. Use a large shallow dish about 4cm deep for best results. Do not cover rice while cooking, but do stir at least twice during cooking.

chapatis

PREPARATION TIME 20 MINUTES (plus standing time) • COOKING TIME 25 MINUTES

2 cups atta flour (320g)
1/2 teaspoon salt
3/4 cup water (180ml), approximately

1 Sift flour and salt into large bowl; add enough water to mix to a firm
 dough. Knead dough on floured surface for 5 minutes. Place dough in
 medium bowl; cover, stand for 1 hour. Divide dough into 12 portions.
 Knead each portion; roll on floured surface into thin rounds about
 16cm in diameter.

2 Place one chapati in heated greased large frying pan; cook over
 medium heat until chapati bubbles and is lightly browned underneath.
 Turn chapati; cook until browned, pressing flat with large spoon
 while cooking. Repeat with remaining chapatis.

MAKES 12

per chapati 0.6g fat; 312kJ

tip Chapatis are best made just before serving time, although they
can be made several hours ahead. Reheat in foil in moderate oven for
about 10 minutes.

Rolling out dough portions

Cooking chapati in pan

Rolling out dough into rounds

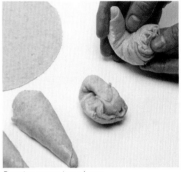

Pressing cones into shape

paratha

PREPARATION TIME 25 MINUTES (plus standing time) • COOKING TIME 10 MINUTES

2 cups atta flour (320g)
30g ghee
²/₃ cup water (160ml),
    approximately
60g ghee, melted, extra
ghee for shallow-frying

1 Sift flour into large bowl; rub in ghee. Make well in centre; stir in enough water to mix to a firm dough. Turn dough onto floured surface; knead for 10 minutes. Cover; stand for 1 hour. Divide dough into eight portions; shape each portion into a ball. Roll on floured surface into rounds about 15cm in diameter.

2 Brush extra ghee over each round. Cut from centre of each round to the outer edge. Starting at one cut edge, roll dough into a cone shape. Press top and bottom of cone towards the centre. Repeat with remaining rounds. Gently roll cones on floured surface into rounds about 15cm in diameter. Shallow-fry rounds in hot ghee until lightly browned on both sides.

MAKES 8

per paratha 17.8g fat; 1208kJ

tip Parathas can be prepared several hours ahead; reheat, covered, in moderate oven for about 3 minutes or until heated through. Store wrapped in a clean cloth.

cumin and chilli puffs

PREPARATION TIME 20 MINUTES (plus standing time) • COOKING TIME 10 MINUTES

**1 cup wholemeal plain
    flour (160g)**
1/2 cup white plain flour (75g)
1/2 teaspoon chilli powder
1 teaspoon cumin seeds
**1/2 cup warm water (125ml),
    approximately**
oil for deep-frying

1 Sift flours and chilli into medium bowl; stir in seeds. Make well in centre; stir in enough water to mix to a soft dough. Turn dough onto floured surface; knead until smooth. Cover; stand for 10 minutes. Divide dough into 12 portions. Shape each portion into a thin sausage about 1cm x 6cm. Coil sausages, flatten with palm of hand.

2 Roll flattened coils on floured surface into rounds about 10cm in diameter. Deep-fry rounds in hot oil, turning once, until golden brown and puffed. Drain on absorbent paper.

MAKES 12

per puff 2.1g fat; 313kJ

tip Puffs can be cooked up to an hour ahead; reheat in moderate oven for about 2 minutes.

Coiling sausages of dough

Rolling flattened coil into round

naan

PREPARATION TIME 25 MINUTES (plus standing time) • COOKING TIME 12 MINUTES

This bread is also known as Punjabi leavened bread.

7g sachet dried yeast
1 teaspoon sugar
1/2 cup warm water (125ml)
3¹/2 cups plain flour (525g)
2 teaspoons sugar, extra
1/4 cup plain yogurt (60ml)
1/4 cup warm water (60ml), extra
1/2 teaspoon ground cumin
1 egg, beaten lightly
60g ghee, melted
2 teaspoons salt
1/2 cup plain yogurt
   (125ml), extra
2 tablespoons poppy seeds

1 Combine yeast, sugar, the water and 1/2 cup of the flour in small bowl; stir until smooth. Cover; stand in warm place for about 10 minutes or until mixture is foamy. Sift remaining flour and extra sugar into large bowl; make well in centre. Pour yeast mixture into dry ingredients. Stir in yogurt, the extra water, cumin, egg, ghee and salt. Turn dough onto floured surface; knead for about 7 minutes or until dough is smooth and elastic. Place dough into lightly greased large bowl; cover. Stand in a warm place for about 45 minutes or until dough has doubled in size.

2 Knead dough until smooth. Divide dough into eight portions; roll portions into balls. Cover; stand for 5 minutes. Roll balls on floured surface into rounds about 15cm in diameter. Spread extra yogurt over each round; sprinkle with poppy seeds. Place rounds on lightly greased oven trays; stand for 5 minutes. Bake in moderately hot oven for about 12 minutes or until browned and crisp.

MAKES 8

per naan 11g fat; 1460kJ
tip Naan is best made close to serving time.

Pouring yeast mixture into dry ingredients

Spreading extra yogurt over rounds

desserts

Asian and Indian desserts are not usually offered after a meal, as they are reserved for special occasions. Instead, daily meals are finished with fresh fruit. Although the recipes in this section are traditional, they have been modified to suit everyone's tastes.

pistachio and brazil nut kulfi

PREPARATION TIME 15 MINUTES (plus cooling and freezing time) • COOKING TIME 20 MINUTES

400g can sweetened
   condensed milk
1 cup coconut cream (250ml)
1 cup cream (250ml)
2 tablespoons grated orange rind
1/2 cup orange juice (125ml)
1/4 cup chopped pistachios (35g)
1/4 cup shredded coconut (15g)
4 cloves
1/4 cup chopped brazil nuts (35g)

1 Combine milk, coconut cream and cream in medium saucepan, stir in rind and juice. Stir over low heat for 3 minutes (or microwave on HIGH for 2 minutes). Stir in pistachios.

2 Stir in coconut and cloves; stir over low heat for 3 minutes (or microwave on HIGH for 2 minutes).

3 Stir in brazil nuts; stir over medium heat for about 15 minutes (or microwave on HIGH for about 12 minutes) or until mixture boils and thickens. Remove from heat; cool for 5 minutes. Remove cloves.

4 Pour mixture into deep loaf pan; cool to room temperature. Cover; freeze for about 2 hours or until almost firm. Remove from freezer, turn mixture into large bowl. Beat with electric mixer until mixture is creamy; return mixture to pan. Cover; freeze until firm.

SERVES 6

per serve 32.6g fat; 2124kJ

tip Kulfi is best made 2 days ahead; store, covered, in freezer.

Stirring rind into mixture

Adding coconut and cloves to mixture

Pouring mixture into pan

coconut crème caramels

PREPARATION TIME 10 MINUTES (plus refrigeration and cooling time) • COOKING TIME 35 MINUTES

400g can coconut cream
1/3 cup milk (80ml)
3 eggs
1/3 cup caster sugar (75g)
1 cup desiccated coconut (90g)
1/2 cup water (125ml)
1/2 cup caster sugar (110g), extra

1 Bring coconut cream and milk to boil in small saucepan; pour mixture into heatproof jug. Whisk eggs and sugar together in medium bowl; gradually whisk in hot coconut cream mixture.

2 Strain mixture into large jug; stir in coconut.

3 Combine the water and extra sugar in small saucepan. Stir over low heat, without boiling, until sugar is dissolved; bring to boil. Boil, uncovered, without stirring, for about 5 minutes or until toffee turns golden brown. Remove from heat.

4 Pour a little toffee into six moulds (1/2-cup capacity); pour coconut mixture over toffee. Place moulds in small baking dish; pour in enough boiling water to come halfway up sides of moulds. Bake in moderate oven for about 20 minutes or until caramels are just set. Remove from water; cool to room temperature. Refrigerate overnight before serving.

SERVES 6

per serve 26.5g fat; 1640kJ

tip Dessert is best made a day ahead; store, covered, in refrigerator.

Whisking in coconut cream mixture

Straining mixture into jug

Pouring toffee into moulds

semolina halwa

PREPARATION TIME 10 MINUTES (plus refrigeration and cooling time) • COOKING TIME 20 MINUTES

¹/₂ cup sugar (110g)
¹/₂ cup milk (125ml)
1 cup water (250ml)
125g butter
2 tablespoons slivered almonds
¹/₂ cup fine semolina (80g)
2 tablespoons sultanas
¹/₂ teaspoon ground cardamom
¹/₂ teaspoon ground cinnamon
2 tablespoons packaged
   ground almonds

1 Lightly grease 8cm x 26cm bar pan. Combine sugar, milk and the water in small saucepan; stir over high heat, without boiling, until sugar is dissolved. Bring to boil; remove from heat, cool. Melt butter in medium saucepan; stir in slivered almonds. Stir over medium heat for about 3 minutes or until almonds are golden brown. Sprinkle semolina into butter mixture; stir over medium heat until mixture boils and semolina turns golden brown.

2 Gradually stir in milk mixture; stir over high heat until mixture boils. Reduce heat; simmer, stirring, for about 3 minutes or until mixture is thickened.

3 Stir in sultanas and cardamom; stir over medium heat for 1 minute. Remove from heat.

4 Spread mixture evenly into prepared pan. Combine cinnamon and ground almonds in a small bowl; sprinkle over halwa. Cool to room temperature; refrigerate until firm.

SERVES 6

per serve 22g fat; 1227kJ
tip Halwa can be made 2 days ahead; store, covered, in refrigerator.

Sprinkling semolina into butter mixture

Adding sultanas and cardamom to pan

Topping halwa with cinnamon and almonds

Beating coconut cream into egg mixture

Pouring mixture into pan

mango coconut ice-cream

PREPARATION TIME 15 MINUTES (plus freezing time) • COOKING TIME 5 MINUTES

5 egg yolks
1/2 cup caster sugar (110g)
400ml coconut cream
425g can sliced mangoes, drained
1/3 cup lemon juice (80ml)
300ml thickened cream

1 Beat egg yolks and sugar in small bowl, with electric mixer, until light and fluffy. Bring coconut cream to boil in small saucepan (or microwave on HIGH for 2 minutes). Gradually beat hot coconut cream into egg mixture, while mixer is operating. Transfer mixture to large bowl.

2 Blend or process mangoes and juice until smooth.

3 Beat cream in small bowl until soft peaks form. Fold mango mixture and cream into egg mixture.

4 Pour mixture into loaf pan; cover with foil. Freeze until firm. Serve sprinkled with toasted coconut, if desired.

SERVES 6

per serve 36.7g fat; 2052kJ

tip Recipe can be made 3 days ahead; store, covered, in freezer.

rosewater doughnuts with sweet yogurt

PREPARATION TIME 30 MINUTES • COOKING TIME 50 MINUTES

2¹/₄ cups self-raising flour (335g)
¹/₂ cup packaged ground
    almonds (60g)
90g ghee, melted
¹/₃ cup plain yogurt (80ml)
¹/₄ cup warm water (60ml)
1 teaspoon rosewater
ghee for deep-frying, extra
¹/₃ cup caster sugar (75g)

SWEET YOGURT
1 cup plain yogurt (250ml)
¹/₂ teaspoon rosewater
1 tablespoon icing sugar

1 Combine sifted flour and almonds in large bowl; rub in ghee. Stir in combined yogurt, water and rosewater; mix to a soft dough.

2 Turn dough onto floured surface; knead until smooth. Divide dough into 32 portions; roll portions into balls. Flatten with fingers.

3 Melt extra ghee for deep-frying in medium saucepan; deep-fry doughnuts a few at a time, for about 6 minutes or until golden brown. Remove from pan; drain on absorbent paper.

4 Toss hot doughnuts in caster sugar; serve with sweet yogurt.

sweet yogurt Combine yogurt, rosewater and sifted icing sugar in small bowl; mix well.

SERVES 8

per serve 22.1g fat; 1674kJ

tip Doughnuts are best made close to serving time.

Flattening dough balls with fingers

Deep-frying doughnuts in ghee

Tossing doughnuts in sugar

lime ice-cream

PREPARATION TIME 15 MINUTES (plus cooling and freezing time) • COOKING TIME 5 MINUTES

2 eggs
¹/₂ cup caster sugar (110g)
3 teaspoons custard powder
1³/₄ cups milk (430ml)
1 teaspoon grated lime rind
1 teaspoon gelatine
2 tablespoons lime juice
¹/₂ cup thickened cream (125ml)

1 Beat eggs, sugar and powder in small bowl, with electric mixer, until thick and creamy. Heat milk in medium saucepan, until almost boiling; remove from heat. Gradually whisk hot milk into egg mixture. Return mixture to saucepan; stir over medium heat until mixture boils and thickens. Remove from heat; stir in rind.

2 Sprinkle gelatine over juice in small bowl; stand in small saucepan of simmering water. Stir until dissolved.

3 Stir gelatine mixture into custard. Cover; cool to room temperature.

4 Beat cream until soft peaks form; fold into custard. Pour mixture into loaf pan or freezer tray; cover. Freeze for about 6 hours or until just firm.

5 Remove ice-cream from freezer; chop roughly. Transfer to small bowl; beat with electric mixer until smooth.

6 Return ice-cream to pan; cover. Freeze until firm.

SERVES 6

per serve 12.3g fat; 940kJ

tip Ice-cream can be made 3 days ahead; store, covered, in freezer.

Folding cream into custard

Beating chopped ice-cream in mixer

Returning ice-cream to pan

glossary

Allspice pimento in ground form.

Almonds we used commercially ground packaged almonds, unless otherwise specified.

Baking powder a raising agent; mostly made from cream of tartar and bicarbonate of soda in the proportion of 1 level teaspoon of cream of tartar to 1/2 level teaspoon of bicarbonate of soda. This is equivalent to 2 teaspoons baking powder.

Bamboo skewers can be used instead of metal skewers if they are soaked in water overnight or for several hours beforehand to prevent burning during cooking. They are available in several different lengths.

Beef
CHUCK STEAK cut from the neck of the animal. Flesh is firm, with a coarse grain, red colour and little fat. Recommended for long cooking.
MINCED BEEF ground beef.
TOPSIDE STEAK cut from the hind leg of the animal.

Breadcrumbs
STALE use one- or two-day-old white bread made into crumbs by grating, blending or processing.
PACKAGED use commercially packaged breadcrumbs.

Butter use salted or unsalted (sweet); 125g butter is equal to 1 stick of butter.

Buttermilk the liquid left from cream after separation; is slightly sour to taste. Skim milk can be substituted.

Capsicum also known as bell pepper or, simply, pepper.

Caraway seeds have a slight anise flavour; available as seeds or in ground form.

Cardamom an expensive spice with an exotic fragrance, available in pod, seed or ground form. You can grind your own cardamom from the seeds in a mortar and pestle.

Chicken
MARYLAND joined leg and thigh with skin intact.

THIGH FILLET skinless and boneless fillet cut from the thigh.

Chickpeas also known as garbanzos, hummus or channa. They are a staple food in the Middle East and India. Cover dried peas well with water; stand overnight. Next day, drain, then boil in plenty of water for about 1 hour or until tender.

Chilli powder the Asian variety is the hottest and is made from ground chillies; it can be used as a substitute for fresh chillies in the proportion of 1/2 teaspoon ground chilli powder to 1 medium chopped chilli.

Cider vinegar vinegar made from fermented apples.

Cinnamon fragrant bark used as a spice in ground form or sticks (quills).

Cloves dried flower buds of a tropical tree; can be used whole or in ground form.

Cornflour cornstarch.

Cream
THICKENED (WHIPPING) CREAM is specified when necessary in recipes.
CREAM is simply a light pouring cream, also known as half 'n' half.
REDUCED CREAM a canned product with a 25% fat content.
SOUR CREAM a thick commercially cultured soured cream.
SOUR LIGHT CREAM a less dense commercially cultured sour cream.

Cumin a warm pungent spice used mainly in savoury dishes; available as seeds or in ground form.

Curry leaves available fresh or dried; have a mild curry flavour. Use similarly to bay leaves.

Custard powder pudding mix.

Eggplant also known as aubergine.

Fennel ground fennel or fennel seeds can be a component of curry powder; it has an aniseed taste.

Fenugreek dried seeds are used in curries, pickles and chutneys.

DRIED LIME RIND AND LEAVES

Fish sauce an essential ingredient in the cooking of a number of South-East Asian countries, including Thailand and Vietnam. It is made from the liquid drained from salted, fermented anchovies. It has a very strong smell and taste. Use sparingly until you acquire the taste.

Flour
ATTA also known as continental flour, fine wholewheat flour.
BESAN a flour made from ground chickpeas. It is used as a thickener and as a main ingredient in the cooking of India.
RICE flour made from rice; ground rice can be substituted.
WHITE PLAIN all-purpose flour.
WHITE SELF-RAISING substitute plain (all-purpose) flour and baking powder in the proportion of 3/4 metric cup plain flour to 2 metric teaspoons baking powder. Sift together several times. If using an 8oz measuring cup, use 1 cup plain flour to 2 metric teaspoons baking powder.
WHOLEMEAL wholewheat flour.
WHOLEMEAL SELF-RAISING add baking powder as above to make wholemeal self-raising flour.

Galangal the root of a plant of the ginger family; used as a flavouring.

FRESH AND DRIED GALANGAL

Garam masala varied combinations of cardamom, cinnamon, cloves, coriander, cumin and nutmeg make this spice, which is often used in Indian cooking. Sometimes pepper is used to make a hot variation. Garam masala is available from Asian food stores and most supermarkets. We give a recipe in the curry blends and pastes section of this book.

Green ginger wine an alcoholic sweet wine infused with finely ground ginger.

Green onions also known as scallion or (incorrectly) shallot; an immature onion picked before the bulb has formed, having a long, bright-green edible stalk.

Herbs
GROUND use powdered form.
DRIED LEAVES use dehydrated herb.
FRESH if unavailable, use a quarter of the dried leaf variety instead of the fresh; for example, use 1 teaspoon dried basil leaves as a substitute for 1 tablespoon (4 teaspoons) chopped fresh basil. This is not recommended when more than a tablespoon of fresh herbs is to be substituted in individual recipes.

Lentils many varieties of dried legumes, identified and named after their colour. Most require overnight soaking before cooking.

Lime dried leaves and dried rind are used as flavourings; substitute strips of fresh lemon or lime rind.

Lobster also known as crayfish.

Milk
SWEETENED CONDENSED made from fresh cow milk with approximately 60% of the water removed by evaporation; sugar is then added.

Mint a tangy aromatic herb available fresh or dried.

Mushrooms, Shiitake dried mushrooms having a unique flavour; soak in hot water, covered, for 20 minutes, drain. Remove and discard stems, use caps as indicated in recipes.

Mustard seeds tiny seeds used in curries, pickling and making mustard; seeds can be black, brown and yellow.

Nutmeg the dried nut of an evergreen tree native to Indonesia; it is available in ground form or you can grate your own with a fine grater.

Oil

PEANUT OIL made from ground peanuts; the most commonly used oil in Asian cooking. A lighter salad-type oil can be substituted.

SESAME OIL made from roasted, crushed white sesame seeds; an aromatic golden-coloured oil with a nutty flavour. It is always used in small quantities and added mostly towards the end of the cooking time. It is not the same as the sesame oil sold in health food stores and should not be used to fry food. It is a flavouring only and can be bought in supermarkets and Asian food stores.

Oyster sauce a rich brown sauce made from oysters cooked in salt and soy sauce, then thickened with different types of starches.

Paprika made from ground dried peppers; varies in taste from the mild to hot and sweet, and in appearance from brownish to scarlet.

Peeled split mung beans dried packaged mung beans available from Asian food stores.

Pimento whole allspice.

Poppy seeds tiny black seeds with a pungent flavour; store in an airtight container in a cool place or freeze as they can become rancid.

Pork fillet skinless, boneless eye fillet cut from the loin.

Poultry sizes numbers indicate weight; for example, a chicken or duck weighing 1.5kg is a size 15; 1.3kg is a size 13; 900g is a size 9.

Red onion also known as Spanish, red Spanish or Bermuda onion; large purplish-red onion.

Rice

LONG-GRAIN elongated grains.

SHORT-GRAIN about half the length of long-grain rice, but thicker.

BASMATI has similar appearance to long-grain rice with a fine aroma. Basmati rice should be washed thoroughly in several changes of water before being cooked.

Rosewater an extract made from crushed rose petals.

Saffron the most expensive of all spices, it is available in threads or powder form. It is made from the dried stamens of the crocus flower. The quality of this spice varies greatly.

Sambal djeroek made from lemon juice and Indonesian sour fruits.

Sambal oelek (also uelek or ulek) a paste made from ground chillies and salt; it can be used as an ingredient or as an accompaniment.

Semolina the hard part of the wheat which is sifted out and used mainly for making pasta.

Sesame seeds there are two types, black and white; we used the white variety in this book. They are almost always toasted.

Shrimp paste a powerful dark brown flavouring made from salted dried shrimp.

Silverbeet (spinach) remove coarse white stems, cook green leafy parts as individual recipes indicate.

Split peas, yellow dried peas often used for making soups.

Stock 1 cup stock (250ml) is the equivalent of 1 cup water (250ml) plus 1 crumbled stock cube (or 1 teaspoon stock powder).

Soy sauce made from fermented soy beans; we used the light and dark varieties. The light is generally used with white meat dishes, and the darker variety with red meat dishes. The dark is normally used for colour and the light for flavour.

PALM SUGAR

Sugar
We used coarse granulated table sugar, also known as crystal sugar, unless otherwise specified.

ICING fine and powdery, also known as confectioners' or powdered sugar.

BROWN soft, fine-textured sugar with some molasses remaining.

CASTER fine granulated table sugar.

PALM very fine sugar from the coconut palm. It is sold in cakes, also known as gula jawa, gula melaka and jaggery. Palm sugar can be substituted with brown or black sugar.

Sultanas seedless white raisins.

Tamarind

CONCENTRATE thick paste made from the acid-tasting fruit of the tamarind tree. To dilute follow instructions on packet.

PULP available in packets from Asian food stores. Place required amount in hot water, allow to cool; squeeze pulp as dry as possible and use the flavoured water.

SAUCE if unavailable, soak about 30g dried tamarind in a cup of hot water, stand for 10 minutes, allow to cool, squeeze pulp as dry as possible and use the flavoured water.

Tandoori mix a mixture of spices used as a marinade and baste for grilling and barbecuing. We give a recipe for tandoori mix in the curry blends and pastes section.

Thyme leaves have a warm, herby taste and can be used fresh or dried.

Toasting almonds and shredded coconut can be toasted in the oven; spread evenly onto oven tray, toast in moderate oven for about 5 minutes. Desiccated coconut and sesame seeds toast more evenly by stirring over heat in a heavy pan; the natural oils will brown both ingredients.

Tomato

PUREE is canned, pureed tomatoes (not tomato paste). Use fresh, peeled, pureed tomatoes as a substitute, if preferred.

SAUCE tomato ketchup.

Turmeric the root of a perennial plant belonging to the ginger family. It is dried, then ground, and is a basic ingredient in curry blends. Curry gets its colour from this spice.

Yogurt plain, unflavoured yogurt is used extensively in Indian cooking as a tenderiser, enricher, thickener and dessert ingredient.

Yeast allow 3 teaspoons (7g) dried yeast to 15g compressed yeast.

Zucchini also known as courgette.

DRIED TAMARIND

TAMARIND CONCENTRATE

index

facts + figures

Wherever you live, you'll be able to use our recipes with the help of these easy-to-follow conversions. While these conversions are approximate only, the difference between an exact and the approximate conversion of various liquid and dry measures is minimal and will not affect your cooking results.

dry measures

metric	imperial
15g	½oz
30g	1oz
60g	2oz
90g	3oz
125g	4oz (¼lb)
155g	5oz
185g	6oz
220g	7oz
250g	8oz (½lb)
280g	9oz
315g	10oz
345g	11oz
375g	12oz (¾lb)
410g	13oz
440g	14oz
470g	15oz
500g	16oz (1lb)
750g	24oz (1½lb)
1kg	32oz (2lb)

liquid measures

metric	imperial
30ml	1 fluid oz
60ml	2 fluid oz
100ml	3 fluid oz
125ml	4 fluid oz
150ml	5 fluid oz (¼ pint/1 gill)
190ml	6 fluid oz
250ml	8 fluid oz
300ml	10 fluid oz (½ pint)
500ml	16 fluid oz
600ml	20 fluid oz (1 pint)
1000ml (1 litre)	1¾ pints

helpful measures

metric	imperial
3mm	⅛in
6mm	¼in
1cm	½in
2cm	¾in
2.5cm	1in
5cm	2in
6cm	2½in
8cm	3in
10cm	4in
13cm	5in
15cm	6in
18cm	7in
20cm	8in
23cm	9in
25cm	10in
28cm	11in
30cm	12in (1ft)

measuring equipment

The difference between one country's measuring cups and another's is, at most, within a 2 or 3 teaspoon variance. (For the record, one Australian metric measuring cup holds approximately 250ml.) The most accurate way of measuring dry ingredients is to weigh them. When measuring liquids, use a clear glass or plastic jug with the metric markings. (One Australian metric tablespoon holds 20ml; one Australian metric teaspoon holds 5ml.)

how to measure

When using graduated metric measuring cups, shake dry ingredients loosely into the appropriate cup. Do not tap the cup on a bench or tightly pack the ingredients unless directed to do so. Level top of measuring cups and measuring spoons with a knife. When measuring liquids, place a clear glass or plastic jug with metric markings on a flat surface to check accuracy at eye level.

Note: North America, NZ and the UK use 15ml tablespoons. All cup and spoon measurements are level.

We use large eggs having an average weight of 60g.

oven temperatures

These oven temperatures are only a guide. Always check the manufacturer's manual.

	°C (Celsius)	°F (Fahrenheit)	Gas Mark
Very slow	120	250	½
Slow	140 – 150	275 – 300	1 – 2
Moderately slow	170	325	3
Moderate	180 – 190	350 – 375	4 – 5
Moderately hot	200	400	6
Hot	220 – 230	425 – 450	7 – 8
Very hot	240	475	9

Looking after **your interest...**

Keep your ACP cookbooks clean, tidy and within easy reach with slipcovers designed to hold up to 12 books. Plus you can follow our recipes perfectly with a set of accurate measuring cups and spoons, as used by *The Australian Women's Weekly* Test Kitchen.

To order

Mail or fax Photocopy and complete the coupon below and post to ACP Books Reader Offer, ACP Publishing, GPO Box 4967, Sydney NSW 2001, or fax to (02) 9267 4967.

Phone Have your credit card details ready, then phone 136 116 (Mon-Fri, 8.00am-6.00pm; Sat, 8.00am-6.00pm).

Price

Book Holder

Australia: $13.10 (incl. GST).
Elsewhere: $A21.95.

Metric Measuring Set

Australia: $6.50 (incl. GST).
New Zealand: $A8.00.
Elsewhere: $A9.95.

Prices include postage and handling.
This offer is available in all countries.

Payment

Australian residents

We accept the credit cards listed on the coupon, money orders and cheques.

Overseas residents

We accept the credit cards listed on the coupon, drafts in $A drawn on an Australian bank, and also British, New Zealand and U.S. cheques in the currency of the country of issue. Credit card charges are at the exchange rate current at the time of payment.

Photocopy and complete coupon below

- -

☐ **Book Holder**

☐ **Metric Measuring Set**
   Please indicate number(s) required.

Mr/Mrs/Ms _____

Address _____

_____

Postcode _____ Country _____

Ph: Business hours (   ) _____

I enclose my cheque/money order for $ _____
payable to ACP Publishing.

OR: please charge my

☐ Bankcard   ☐ Visa   ☐ Mastercard

☐ Diners Club   ☐ American Express

Card number

Expiry date ____ /____

Cardholder's signature _____

Please allow up to 30 days delivery within Australia.
Allow up to 6 weeks for overseas deliveries.
Both offers expire 31/12/05. HLECC04

Test Kitchen Staff
Food director *Pamela Clark*
Assistant food editors *Barbara Northwood, Jan Castor*
Associate food editor *Enid Morrison*
Chief home economist *Kathy Wharton*
Home economists *Jon Allen, Jane Ash, Tikki Durant, Sue Hipwell, Voula Mantzouridis, Karen Maughan, Louise Patniotis*
Stylists *Jon Allen, Rosemary de Santis, Carolyn Fienbe Michelle Gorry, Jacqui Hing, Victoria Lewis, Anna Phillip*
Photographers *Kevin Brown, Robert Clark, Justine Kerrigan, Andre Martin, Georgia Moxham, Robert Taylc Jon Waddy*

ACP Books Staff
Editorial director *Susan Tomnay*
Creative director *Hieu Chi Nguyen*
Senior editor *Lynda Wilton*
Designer *Michele Withers*
Studio manager *Caryl Wiggins*
Editorial/sales coordinator *Caroline Lowry*
Editorial assistant *Karen Lai*
Publishing manager (sales) *Brian Cearnes*
Publishing manager (rights & new projects) *Jane Hazell*
Marketing manager *Sarah Cave*
Pre-press *Harry Palmer*
Production manager *Carol Currie*
Business manager *Seymour Cohen*
Assistant business analyst *Martin Howes*
Chief executive officer *John Alexander*
Group publisher *Pat Ingram*
Publisher *Sue Wannan*
Editor-in-chief *Deborah Thomas*

Produced by ACP Books, Sydney.
Colour separations by ACP Colour Graphics Pty Ltd, Sydney.
Printed by Dai Nippon Printing in Korea.
Published by ACP Publishing Pty Limited, 54 Park St, Sydney; GPO Box 4088, Sydney, NSW 2001.
Ph: (02) 9282 8618 Fax: (02) 9267 9438.
acpbooks@acp.com.au
www.acpbooks.com.au
To order books, phone 136 116.
Send recipe enquiries to recipeenquiries@acp.com.au
AUSTRALIA: Distributed by Network Services, GPO Box 4088, Sydney, NSW 2001.
Ph: (02) 9282 8777 Fax: (02) 9264 3278.
UNITED KINGDOM: Distributed by Australian Consolida Press (UK), Moulton Park Business Centre, Red House Moulton Park, Northampton, NN3 6AQ Ph: (01604) 49 531 Fax: (01604) 497 533 acpukltd@aol.com
CANADA: Distributed by Whitecap Books Ltd, 351 Lynn Ave, North Vancouver, BC, V7J 2C4, Ph: (604) 980 9852.
NEW ZEALAND: Distributed by Netlink Distribution Company, Level 4, 23 Hargreaves St, College Hill, Auckland 1, Ph: (9) 302 7616.
SOUTH AFRICA: Distributed by PSD Promotions, 3(Diesel Road Isando, Gauteng Johannesburg.
PO Box 1175, Isando 1600, Gauteng Johannesbur;
Ph: (2711) 392 6065/6/7
Fax: (2711) 392 6079/80
orders@psdprom.co.za

Easy Curry Cookery
Includes index.
ISBN 0 949892 76 9
   1. Cookery (Curry). (Series: Australian Women's Weekly Home Library).
   641.6384